Salsa, Language and Transnationalism

ENCOUNTERS

Series Editors: **Jan Blommaert**, *Tilburg University, The Netherlands*, **Ben Rampton**, *Kings College London, UK*, **Anna De Fina**, *Georgetown University, USA* and **Marco Jacquemet**, *University of San Francisco, USA*

The Encounters series sets out to explore diversity in language from a theoretical and an applied perspective. So the focus is both on the linguistic encounters, inequalities and struggles that characterise post-modern societies and on the development, within sociocultural linguistics, of theoretical instruments to explain them. The series welcomes work dealing with such topics as heterogeneity, mixing, creolisation, bricolage, cross-over phenomena, polylingual and polycultural practices. Another high-priority area of study is the investigation of processes through which linguistic resources are negotiated, appropriated and controlled, and the mechanisms leading to the creation and maintenance of sociocultural differences. The series welcomes ethnographically oriented work in which contexts of communication are investigated rather than assumed, as well as research that shows a clear commitment to close analysis of local meaning-making processes and the semiotic organisation of texts.

Full details of all the books in this series and of all our other publications can be found on http://www.multilingual-matters.com, or by writing to Multilingual Matters, St Nicholas House, 31–34 High Street, Bristol BS1 2AW, UK.

ENCOUNTERS: 3

Salsa, Language and Transnationalism

Britta Schneider

MULTILINGUAL MATTERS
Bristol • Buffalo • Toronto

Library of Congress Cataloging in Publication Data
A catalog record for this book is available from the Library of Congress.
Schneider, Britta.
Salsa, Language and Transnationalism/Britta Schneider.
Encounters: 3
Includes bibliographical references.
1. Linguistic minorities. 2. Languages in contact. 3. Multiculturalism–Social aspects. 4. Salsa (Music)–Social aspects. 5. Sociolinguistics. 6. Linguistic demography. I. Title.
P40.5.L56S39 2014
306.44–dc23 2014001718

British Library Cataloguing in Publication Data
A catalogue entry for this book is available from the British Library.

ISBN-13: 978-1-78309-189-8 (hbk)
ISBN-13: 978-1-78309-188-1 (pbk)

Multilingual Matters
UK: St Nicholas House, 31-34 High Street, Bristol BS1 2AW, UK.
USA: UTP, 2250 Military Road, Tonawanda, NY 14150, USA.
Canada: UTP, 5201 Dufferin Street, North York, Ontario M3H 5T8, Canada.

Website: www.multilingual-matters.com
Twitter: Multi_Ling_Mat
Facebook: https://www.facebook.com/multilingualmatters
Blog: www.channelviewpublications.wordpress.com

Typeset by R. J. Footring Ltd, Derby
Printed and bound in Great Britain by the CPI Group (UK Ltd), Croydon, CR0 4YY

Contents

Acknowledgements

This book would not have been possible without the support and inspiration of many people. First of all, it would not have been realised with the generous support and assistance of Ben Rampton, who has invited me to publish my project – thank you, Ben!

I will always be grateful to Marlis Hellinger, who brought me into sociolinguistics in the first place, and gave me the freedom and support to delve into unknown territories. I want to thank Martina Möllering, whose interest, assistance and constructive feedback inspired me a lot, and I want to thank Susanne Mühleisen, Jan Blommaert and Alastair Pennycook for invaluable comments on an earlier version of this text.

I am still astonished by the unbureaucratic financial, organisational and moral support that I have been given by Macquarie University; and I want to thank the Dr Hans Messer Sozialstiftung and the International Office of Goethe University Frankfurt, without which I could not have conducted research in Australia, where they financed child-care for my daughter. In particular, I want to thank Beate Braungart and Martin Bickl, who are mainly responsible for the organisation of this.

Special thanks go to my dance and interview partners and to those who have given me access to the world of salsa. I particularly want to thank Daniel Heitzenröder, Anja Hardt, Christoph Wiesner and Maria Papadopoulos. For inspiration, support and company, I want to thank Gisela Engel, Ramona Lenz, Maria Dahm, Vera Williams Tetteh, Kimie Takahashi, Carla Müller-Schulzke, Helena McKenzie, Tina Brüderlin, Ela Weller and Rebecca Riegel, and, of course, my parents. I want to say thank you to all who have cared for my children while I have prepared and written this book. Finally, I want to say *Danke* to Michel, whose company and assistance have guided me over many years, and to Nanna and Ava for their positive spirit and their patience ('I have never met a mummy in the whole wide world who reads as much as you!').

Transcription Conventions

(.)	pause of less than 1 second
(1.5)	pause with indicated length
/	overlapping talk
stréss	rise of tone
strèss	fall of tone
underlined	louder
(word¿)	word difficult to hear, analyst's guess
line break	after utterance unit or pause

1 Salsa, Zombies and Linguistics

We must question those ready-made syntheses, those groupings that we normally accept before any examination, those links whose validity is recognized from the outset; [...]. And instead of according them unqualified, spontaneous value, we must accept, in the name of methodological vigour, that, in the first instance, they concern only a population of dispersed events.
Foucault (1972: 22)

A while ago, a friend of mine gave birth to her second son. He was born in Frankfurt, Germany; accordingly, one may assume that his 'native language' is German. Yet, it is not only the place of birth but also the parents' cultural and linguistic heritage that are taken as indicators for the language considered to be 'native' to a child. In the case of the little boy just mentioned, however, both a territorial and a heritage approach to linguistic identity are problematic. While the mother is 'half' Serbo-Montenegrin and 'half' Hungarian, the father's parents stem from Spain and Greece.

In urban contexts today, linguistic complexities like this are by no means an exception. In Frankfurt, London, New York or Sydney, it has become unexceptional that people from different cultural backgrounds live together, become friends, attend the same schools and love each other. And, thus, affiliations with groups or with patterns of verbal and other behaviour oftentimes do not fit into established frameworks of culture and linguistic identity. However, although multiculturalism and multilingualism have become common, the categories with which culture, language and identity are described often obscure these complexities of social reality. Categories like *cultures*, *nations* or *languages*, categories that describe the world as materialising in static, bounded systems, draw an overly simple picture. Yet, they are still relevant for describing social life. It would be difficult to give an account of multicultural identity, as in the example above, without making reference to the concepts that are put into question through the existence of such identities. The notion of 'zombie category' (Beck, 2001) illustrates this paradoxical situation. *Zombies* are creatures that are dead and alive at the same time.

A concept that is crucial for the continuing relevance of such 'zombies', and that is the focus of this book, is the notion of *language*, in its function of denoting distinct and separate verbal systems. National cultures, for example, are co-defined through languages, and membership of a culture (or a sub-culture thereof) usually depends on language competence. The cultural autonomy of national and ethnic groups is typically legitimised by a *language* that proves their existence, and that is conceptualised as self-contained. Despite this important social function of languages, an understanding of the concept of *language* as a culturally constructed category has received relatively little attention. Even so, like *nation*, *gender* or *class*, the concept of *language*, as describing a distinct structural entity, has not fallen from heaven. *Languages* as bounded entities, marking cultural boundaries, have developed historically and are the result of specific discourses. They are central in imaginations of national cultures and are the result of language ideologies that are historically related to national epistemology and colonialism (see e.g. Errington, 2008; Gal & Irvine, 1995; Irvine, 2001; Irvine & Gal, 2009; Makoni & Pennycook, 2007; Pennycook, 2004; Pratt, 1987).

During the 20th century, the discipline of linguistics tended to regard linguistic systems, understood as separate entities, as fundamental and unquestioned objects of study. Therefore, the analysis of the discursive construction and the study of the cultural, political and social relevance of *languages* have remained somewhat marginal linguistics. Language ideologies that are found in linguistics often implicitly confirm the idea of the existence of culturally and linguistically homogenous groups and usually consider the language use of social elites to be 'a language': 'To speak of *the* language, without further specification, as linguists do, is tacitly to accept the *official* language of a political unit' (Bourdieu, 1980 [2000]: 468). To regard the official language of a nation as basis for research, without questioning its ontological status, is an instance of *methodological nationalism*. Methodological nationalism has been defined as the 'assumption that the nation/state/society is the natural social and political form of the modern world' (Wimmer & Schiller, 2002: 301). Historically, it has developed on the grounds of the fact that '[t]he epistemic structures and programmes of mainstream social sciences have been closely attached to, and shaped by, the experience of modern nation-state formation' (Wimmer & Schiller, 2002: 303).

In an age of globalisation, it has become apparent that nations, cultures and languages are no 'natural' entities. Yet, how can we talk about such 'zombie' categories without giving them a 'natural' status? How can we conceptualise language and identity in a world in which the connection between culture and language is no longer as straightforward as it seemed to be in the past? How can we use the concept of *language* without assuming that there are fixed communities to which languages are 'naturally' tied? To develop an understanding of how languages and their symbolic functions are constituted in discourse is central to grasp their role in the creation of community and society in a post-national context. The study presented in this volume is an attempt to get a hesitant glimpse of the contemporary discursive constitution of languages, assuming that the *language–culture* nexus needs to be put into question. Due to the relevance of these questions in many realms, I regard not only linguists, sociolinguists and linguistic anthropologists as the potential audience of this book but consider to be a potential a reader anyone who has an interest in the role of language in a transnational world. This involves above all cultural anthropologists, but also students and scholars of sociology, of political sciences and of cultural studies, and teachers in urban classrooms who want to get a closer understanding of the ideologies underlying the language practices of their multilingual pupils.

Transnational Salsa – The Object of Study

In approaching language in an age of globalisation empirically, I will try to avoid *methodological nationalism*. The study presented therefore focuses on language ideologies in transnational social formations that are not based on ethnicity. Instead of choosing an ethnic or national group as the object of study, communities based on salsa dance, located in Australia and in Germany, are the focus. Their language ideologies – their discourses and beliefs about language – are at the centre of attention. Such a choice is slightly unusual in a linguistic study and requires explanation.

First of all, popular music in general, in production and consumption, has a strong tendency to produce transnational ties (see e.g. Lipsitz, 1994: 4). With their history of cultural mixing, popular music and dance styles are inspiring examples for the study of discourses *between* cultures, languages and spaces. As such, salsa dancing is a globally popular cultural activity. From Japan to Greece, from Canada to Senegal, salsa clubs are found all over the world. Cultural studies (see e.g. Hall, 1992; Rampton, 1997; Williams, 1966) have emphasised the need to look into the practices of everyday life, influenced by capitalist mass culture, not necessarily tied to ethnicity. In the everyday life of contemporary societies, cultural practices based on music, connected to commercialism, the production of lifestyle and mass media are at least as common as more traditional activities that reproduce social orders such as ethnic or national identity. Studying communities based on commercial music culture is not a random and exotic choice but is anchored in the development of contemporary capitalist culture. Leisure culture related to music, like the activity of dancing salsa, is an essential part of everyday discourse and influences the way people locate themselves – and thus also the way they use and conceptualise language.

Secondly, salsa brings along local ethnic mixing, as there are many dancers in salsa communities who relate to the dance due to their cultural heritage, as well as even more whose ethnic heritage is completely unrelated to salsa. The latter group includes local majority populations (in the study presented here, 'German' Germans, Anglo-Australians), as well as a large number of members of ethnic minority groups, for example Turkish, Sudanese, Arab or Greek in the case of Germany, or Chinese, Vietnamese, southern European, Lebanese and other Arab dancers in the case of Australia. Salsa communities are therefore an interesting example to use to study 'the operation of language across lines of social differentiation', related to the idea that linguistics should focus 'on modes and zones of contact' (Pratt, 1987: 60) instead of engaging in a 'linguistics of community' (Pratt, 1987: 49) that assumes that language emerges from ethnicity (see also Chapter 2).

Finally, despite the transnational connections that can and do develop on the grounds of salsa, it is still very often seen as 'ethnic', namely as a more or less 'Latin' or 'Hispanic' cultural practice.[1] As a consequence of this, the activity of dancing salsa typically involves certain language(-listening) practices, as salsa music is mostly sung in Spanish. And, interestingly, salsa often not only leads to people listening to music with Spanish lyrics. In the contexts observed in this study, there are quite a number of people of non-Hispanic descent who enthusiastically identify with the Spanish language. Thus, globally popular salsa communities, with their transnational Latin and mixed origins, their many non-ethnic Spanish-speaking members and their ethnically hybrid constitution, form an interesting case for studying language ideologies in a transnational environment, in which issues related to language and ethnicity remain nevertheless significant.[2]

The type of identity that is constructed in salsa communities is obviously different from, for example, gender or ethnicity. However, it is its precarious, temporary and also consumerist nature, different from 'traditional' conceptions of identity, which makes salsa and its discourses interesting for studying the development of language ideology in a capitalist culture with transnational connections. While stability and order have been tacit assumptions of studies of the social in structuralist approaches,

> [r]andomness and disorder have [...] become much more important in recent social theory, where instead of trying to define the core features of any social group or institution, there is major interest in the flows of people, knowledge, texts and objects across social and geographical space, in the boundaries of inclusion and exclusion, and in fragmentation, indeterminacy and ambivalence. (Rampton, 2000b: 11)

Despite a recognition of the precariousness of cultures and identities, one should be aware that national discourses are still decisive factors in everyday life and determine very real boundaries and identities. Cross-national comparison allows for a visibility of national discourses and for a study of the influence of national discourse and language policies on localised transnational culture (see also Hornberger, 2005). The two countries chosen for the present study, Germany and Australia, have very different histories and ideologies of citizenship and belonging. Germany, with a tradition of national ideologies of belonging, contrasts with Australia as an immigrant nation, where the official acknowledgement of diversity has a much longer history. Studying salsa communities in different countries therefore generates insights into non-essentialised, non-ethnic forms of language identity, without losing sight of the potentially continuing relevance of ethnic and national discourse and language.

Overcoming Linguistic Essentialism

One inspiration to study transnationalism and language is of an intellectual nature, as it means to question and analyse the constitution and ontological status of the concept of *language*. On the other hand, the underlying motivation of this study is linked to ethical demands. Racial and cultural discrimination is often reconstructed and made possible on the basis of linguistic differences. '[T]he ethical demand to imagine *otherwise*' (Kearney, 1988: 364, quoted in Pennycook, 2001: 154) leads to an interrogation of the idea that each culture is tied to one language. In academic and educational discourses concerned with discrimination based on language, the connection between a culture and 'its' language is often constructed as self-evident (see e.g. Gogolin & Reich, 2001; Hamel, 1997; Phillipson & Skutnabb-Kangas, 1999; Skutnabb-Kangas, 2000). This can be an important strategy in constructing a 'voice' in the political arena of education in multicultural and multilingual contexts. 'Strategic essentialism' (Spivak, 1996 [1985]) is crucial to make arguments accessible to the public, to politicians and to other policy designers in a world in which the majority of nations are still reluctant to meet the requirements of basic language rights as demanded by Unesco as early as 1953 (e.g. the right to become literate in one's native language; Unesco, 1953).

Thinking of the little boy introduced above, however, an understanding of the connection between language and culture as 'given' can be problematic for quite practical reasons. It is not possible to say which language is the boy's 'native' language and maybe he will not identify most closely with one of his parents' languages. In such cases, which are no longer exceptions, linguistic essentialism, assuming that people have to 'stick to who they are' (see Djité, 2006), can be a form of symbolic violence. In an age of globalisation, where new identities are formed and hybrid cultures develop, conceptualisations that assume that people simply reproduce their parents' culture and language become particularly controversial. It is crucial to understand that – next to the language–culture nexus – there are other local, national or transnational discourses to which a *language* can be connected.

If, for example, the little boy's mother does not use Hungarian because no one in her environment uses the language, because she has never learned it, or because it is linked to lower-class immigrant status in her local context, it is not very likely that Hungarian will become a dominant language for her son. On the other hand, the global dominance of English, the recent popularity of Spanish in popular culture, or a family stay abroad in Brazil or Japan, for example, may have an impact on his identity formation and language practices. Thus, it is many different discourses, related to ethnic heritage, social networks, political positionings, working conditions and consumerist practices that affect linguistic identity in many present-day contexts. Reducing people to their parents' ethnic and linguistic heritage, even with the best of intentions, not only creates an unrealistic picture but furthermore runs danger of unwillingly excluding, stigmatising or 'othering' people on the grounds of their heritage.

Studying language ideologies in salsa communities aims at documenting newer forms of social positioning and thus at getting a glimpse of the discursive regimes beyond nationalism that are operating in contemporary, globalised societies. The study thus indirectly asks whether, through new forms of social structure, new forms of social knowledge have developed. The overall aim of studying language ideologies in transnational salsa contexts is therefore to document the discourses that influence the choice and conception of *languages*. In order to do this, certain methodological choices are demanded.

Methodological Approach

Basically, this is a study of what language means to people and how this is linked to the discourses they routinely engage in. As this interest is not quantitative in nature but rather aims at understanding meaning-making practices on a local level, and their ties to more widespread discursive regimes, a qualitative, ethnographic approach forms the core methodological choice. The ethnographic method allows access to cultural contexts and insiders' views on a particular culture in order to understand situated behaviour (see e.g. Geertz, 1973; Gobo, 2008). In considering the perspective of 'insiders', ethnography furthermore allows for the inclusion of the 'voice' (Blommaert, 2005: ch. 4) of those who are the focus of research. It is the goal of ethnography to provide an 'emic' perspective, rather than an 'etic' one.[3]

One tool with which to gain access to this perspective is observation. Observation is the 'primary source of information' of ethnography (Gobo, 2008: 5). A particular form of observation that is used in ethnography is participant observation. This requires the researcher to become a quasi-member of a community for a certain period of time Through the experience of being an 'as if' member, a researcher can gain insights into the community that would have been impossible to obtain otherwise and can observe everyday experience and small-scale details of normalised routines, which are often unconscious and therefore would not appear in quantitative interviews or questionnaires. After attending sites of observation, the researcher documents experiences and observations in field notes. Field notes provide valuable insights into cultural practices, but are themselves interpretations and thus have to be approached as cultural constructions, rather than as simple 'facts' (Geertz, 1983a: 22–23). Researchers link their observational data to broader cultural contexts and to social theory. Ideally, the experience of being a quasi-member through participant observation leads to what is called a 'thick description': a constant combination of descriptive details, contextual observation and theorising on broader cultural structures (Geertz, 1973).

It is not only the observation of cultural practices within a community that requires ethnographic methodolgy: discovering non-ethnic, previously undocumented social formations also relies on observational techniques, as does establishing them as research objects. As Figure 1.1 shows, there are many different transnational, non-ethnic communities that can be detected in contemporary consumer culture. It is conceived that these communities come into being through the practices they engage in, but that they are at the same time linked to and constituted in broader discourses (see Chapter 2). Their existence can be confirmed only by ethnographic observation.

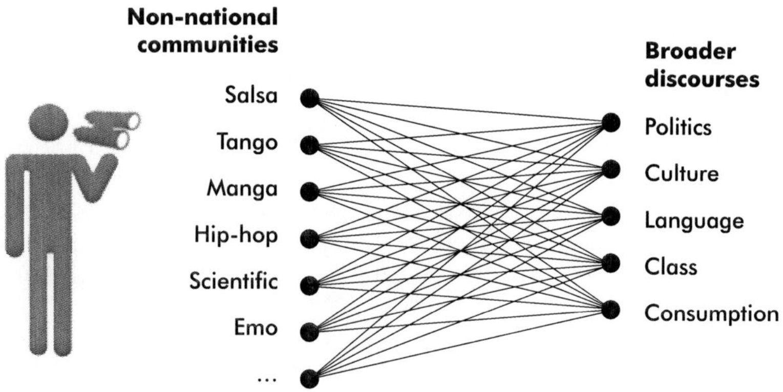

Figure 1.1 Ethnographic approaches to transnational communities and discourses

This holds true for the present study (Box 1.1). I have determined salsa communities as a relevant object of study through online and offline field observations (see also below in this chapter). In contrast to traditional ethnographic fieldwork, however, where researchers stay in the field for several months or even years in order to conduct participant observation, I have not remained in the field for long consecutive periods of time. The nature of contemporary culture makes traditional fieldwork difficult or even impossible, as 'post-traditional communities' (Pfadenhauer, 2005), including salsa communities, do not exist all the time in one particular place. Rather, they are of a more fluid nature, as they come into being only at certain times in certain places. The study presented here thus does not give an anthropological insight into the lives of members of a culture but makes use of ethnographic fieldwork and qualitative methods in order to document a post-traditional

Box 1.1 Field study

- I studied salsa communities for a period of four years. As salsa parties and classes do not take place every day and do not last all day, I usually conducted fieldwork once or twice a week, in salsa clubs and salsa dance schools.
- I conducted 20 qualitative interviews with members of different salsa communities: with 12 lay salsa dancers, two owners of dance schools, five salsa teachers and one salsa DJ.

context and its discourses. As not all discourses in a community become visible through observation and participant observation, these techniques were supplemented by interviews.

The analysis of interviews was inspired by discourse analysis (see Chapter 2) and linguistic ethnography (Rampton *et al.*, 2004). The latter approach links ethnographic insights, which focus on broad social issues, with analytical tools provided by different strands of linguistics. It is argued that ethnography and linguistics can benefit from each other, as ethnography profits from the analytical preciseness of linguistics and linguistics gains from the 'reflexive sensitivity required in ethnography' (Creese, 2008: 232). In analysing interviews in later chapters, I thus interpret not only the content of utterances but also, if relevant, their linguistic form.

In contrast to data-focused approaches like, for example, conversation analysis, it is typical for linguistic ethnography to draw connections between the data and concepts that have been developed in different strands of social science (Rampton, 2006: 404). The approach thus aligns with Clifford Geertz's aim of a 'thick description' (see above), as broad societal structures can be related to small-scale ethnographic and discursive detail. The study can also be considered to be a form of an 'extended case' in Burawoy's understanding. The extended case method 'applies reflexive science to ethnography in order to extract the general from the unique, to move from the "micro" to the "macro," and to connect the present to the past in anticipation of the future, all by building on preexisting theory' (Burawoy, 1998: 5). Theoretical knowledge and social *a priori* knowledge have crucially inspired the research design. This includes, for example, the questioning of the language–culture nexus, the scrutinising of the concept of *language*, and the hypothesis that transnational social structures may bring about new forms of social knowledge about language.

Pre-existing assumptions from social knowledge and the social sciences are also co-responsible for the cross-national research design of the study, which is based on the hypothesis that local discourses may be affected by national contexts. As has been mentioned, salsa communities in two different countries – Germany and Australia – have been studied, in what can be regarded as a form of multi-sited ethnography. Multi-sited ethnography follows the trajectories of people or objects as they travel across sites (Marcus, 1998). In the present case, I document salsa dance in different local and national environments; however, the choice of the different contexts is not based on literal trajectories between Frankfurt and Sydney. The choice of these two national contexts was based on an interest in the impact of national discourses on language in an age of globalisation. Such an approach may tacitly co-construct national discourses, and can be accused of being an instance of methodological nationalism (see above). However, while any cross-national approach reconstructs the nation as a meaningful entity, the existence of legislation on citizenship, visa regulations, language policies and the accompanying discourses in public media do have an impact, which is also confirmed in my data set.

The decision to choose salsa culture in Frankfurt and Sydney as examples for illustrating transnational language ideologies is thus partly based on theoretical assumptions but partly also arose from the acts of fortune that ethnographic research brings along. Originally, I had planned to study the effects of national language policies on individual constructions of linguistic identity in the German, more nationalist context, and in the Australian one, which scientific literature sometimes characterises as having rather inclusive language policies (Lo Bianco, 2008; Phillipson & Skutnabb-Kangas, 1997). Due to my background in Latin American studies and knowledge of Spanish, I first envisaged a study of Latin Americans in both countries. Yet, as I also intended to overcome essentialist approaches to language and identity and wanted to incorporate newer theoretical developments on performativity and constructionist approaches to linguistic identity (see e.g. Pennycook, 2004), the choice of a group based on ethnic descent or citizenship was not very satisfactory.

When I tried to solve the problem, I started to conduct Google searches to get an idea of the activities of Spanish-speaking groups in both countries. Whenever I entered the search term 'Latino' or 'Latin', I had thousands of hits on salsa. It was virtually impossible not to end with salsa when looking for Latin American culture in Frankfurt or Sydney, which I regarded as meaningful. My salsa-dancing, Spanish-speaking friends came to my mind. When I began to conduct research, I had lived in Frankfurt for about eight years and knew several people who were engaged in the salsa scene. All people I knew who danced salsa had travelled to Latin American countries and spoke Spanish; indeed, all of them were fluent in the language. Influenced by cultural anthropological literature on transnationalism (see e.g. Papadopoulos, 2003), I wondered whether these salsa communities might be an illustrative example for transnational culture and therefore an interesting choice for studying the effects of globalisation on language ideology. I had no idea where this would lead me and whether everybody else might think that I was out of my mind to study salsa when I wanted to know something about language. Fortunately, the study brought about highly interesting data on the interaction of global, national and local discourses and their effects on ideologies of language.

The diversity of local appropriations of salsa is one reason for the appeal of the data. The appropriation of salsa is always a local issue but is interwoven with (the sometimes rather conservative) imaginations of the cultural 'other', which tie in with global and national discourses and also have to do with the presence of different styles of salsa in particular cities/places (see Chapter 3 on salsa styles). An ethnographic approach to these locally diverse environments gives insight into the small-scale meaning-making processes and broader social relationships of local actors. An understanding of these is necessary to understand the symbolic meanings of languages, the *language ideologies* of particular communities.

These particular salsa communities are conceptualised as *communities of practice* in the context of this study (Box 1.2). The notion of community of practice allows essentialist theories of belonging to be overcome (such theories are found in studies that take ethnic or national communities as an unproblematised starting point). The term *community of practice* derives from educational studies and was originally used to describe learning through participation (Lave & Wenger, 1991). Three basic features define such a community. The most crucial one is that it is a joint enterprise in which members participate (Holmes & Meyerhoff, 1999: 175; Meyerhoff, 2003: 6). In the case introduced here, this enterprise is, obviously, salsa dancing. The second feature is mutual engagement and regular interaction; the third one is the development of a shared repertoire (Holmes & Meyerhoff, 1999: 175), which is here a shared repertoire of language ideologies.

Box 1.2 The communities of practice

- In total, I determined and studied three different communities of practice and one chapter will be devoted to each of these. While I found only one community of practice in Frankfurt (Chapter 4), I detected two different ones in Sydney, one linked to LA-style salsa (Chapter 5) and one to Cuban-style salsa (Chapter 6). Each community produces different language ideologies.

During the ethnographic fieldwork and my activities as a participant observant, I was, above all, interested in the role of the Spanish language in these communities and in the discursive networks in which language ideologies in transnational contexts are embedded. This related to observations on the oppositions and social boundaries (including and beyond ethnic ones) that are created by the means of symbolic functions of language. In other words, I wanted to know 'how boundaries happen: how people and practices get included and excluded, and what happens to them and to the categories as a result' (Heller, 2007b: 342).

Research Questions and Structure of the Book

The interest in these topics is formulated in three research questions, which have guided the overall research process, and lead through the following chapters on the analysis of empirical data (Chapters 4–6):

(1) Which language ideologies are found in salsa communities?
(2) Next to national language discourses, which other societal or cultural discourses co-constitute language ideologies in salsa communities?
(3) What happens to the notion of *language* in language discourse in a transnational context?

The next chapter, Chapter 2, introduces the theoretical approach to language ideologies and introduces in more detail the notions of *discourse*, *language ideology* and *transnationalism*. In Chapter 3, I give some background information on salsa – its history, development and main features, including the role of ethnic boundaries and of gender as found in the observed contexts. In Chapters 4–6, I introduce discourses and language ideologies of different salsa communities. Chapter 4 is devoted to the community that I detected in Frankfurt, Germany, while Chapters 5 and 6 each introduce one of the communities that I found in Sydney, Australia. Chapters 4 and 5 both begin by setting out the societal background of the German and Australian salsa communities, respectively. Thereafter all three empirical chapters (4–6) follow a similar structure, presenting some general ethnographic observations and observations on language, and then a detailed interpretation of selected interview quotes.

Chapter 7 returns to more theoretical concerns. The chapter generalises on the discourses that come into play and interact in local meaning-making processes. The interaction of discourses from different geographical levels seems to be a crucial aspect of the formation of contemporary language ideologies. Secondly, the notion of *language* and its relevance in a transnational age, with post-national forms of community, are scrutinised. *Languages* remain important analytical categories but relate to a multiplicity of social boundaries, instead of being signifiers of nation or ethnicity only. This discussion is linked to contemporary sociolinguistic theory and to debates on *reflexive modernity* (Beck *et al.*, 2003), as the changing role of language is indicative of overall changes in the framing of modernist categories in globalised societies. It can be assumed that we will have to deal with modernist *zombies* and transnational *salsas* in our everyday lives in the future, and to get a glimpse of what this might mean is the intention of the following chapters.

Notes

(1) Yet, it is important to note that the historical development of salsa is itself transnational – see Chapter 3.
(2) In this sense, salsa is different from other forms of transnational leisure activities like yoga, t'ai chi or origami.
(3) The terms 'etic' and 'emic' have been developed in analogy with phon*etic* and phon*emic* perspectives on sounds in a given language (Pike, 1954).

2 Transnational Language Discourse

> *[O]ther sciences are provided with objects of study in advance, which are then examined from different points of view. Nothing like that is the case in linguistics.*
> Saussure (1913 [1993]: 8)

For non-specialists, but also for many structural linguists, an ethnography of salsa communities as a linguistic study represents at best a marginal, at worst a mistaken choice. At first sight, the study of linguistics seems to be easy to define. A linguist studies language. A central assumption of the study presented here is that establishing the object of research in linguistics is a challenging task. What actually is *a language*? What do we study if we study *language*? There are many different answers to these questions. They depend on the particular interest in language one has and on how the verbal performance of human beings is conceptualised. Conceptions of languages are also called *language ideologies* and these are the central focus of this volume. In a more theoretical vein, language ideologies can be regarded as *discourses*. A discursive understanding of language is based on the idea that what people, including linguists, think about language comes into being through discursive acts, such as speaking or writing.

In the following, I first lay the foundation for a post-structuralist perspective on discourse. Afterwards, I focus on aspects pertaining to discourses on language – *language ideologies* – where national ideologies of language, which conceptualise a connection between language and culture, take a particularly prominent place. Finally, as this study investigates language ideologies in transnational contexts, I introduce the notion of transnationalism. I then briefly explain the related idea of cosmopolitanism, and present some relevant concepts for non-structuralist views of language. These concepts form the theoretical basis for the empirical analysis of language discourse in transnational salsa communities, in Chapters 4–6.

Discourse Theory

Confusingly, *discourse* is an umbrella term for many different strands of linguistic and social theory (see e.g. Blommaert, 2005; Cameron, 2001; Foucault, 1972 [2001]; Foucault, 1970 [2000]; Gee, 2005; Geller, 2005; Jaworski & Coupland, 2006; McHoul, 2001; Mills, 1997). Nevertheless, there are some basic assumptions that these approaches share. One feature that is agreed upon is that 'discourse' refers to language use above the sentence level (Cameron, 2001: 10). Many linguistic studies of discourse are, for example, interested in formal structures of larger stretches of text (see e.g. Paltridge, 2006: ch. 6). In more functionally oriented approaches, it is seen as crucial that language can in fact itself constitute social reality. Language is here regarded as a means to act in the social world. Performative speech acts are a prominent example of the power of language to change social reality (for example the sentence 'I hereby declare you husband and wife', as presented in just about any introductory textbook on pragmatics).

The idea that language co-constructs social reality became prominent in non-linguistic sciences during the 1960s (for an early account, see Berger & Luckmann, 1966). Michel Foucault is one of the most prolific and also most often-quoted scholars in this context (see e.g. Foucault, 1970, 1970 [2000], 1972, 1979, 1980a, 1980b). Similar to what has been said above, the idea of the constitutive nature of language in Foucault's writings goes beyond the level of single speech acts. In this understanding, all aspects of the social world are related to and rely on language – on *discourse* – as 'discourse is beyond language in use. Discourse is language use relative to social, political and cultural formations – it is language reflecting social order but also language shaping social order' (Jaworski & Coupland, 2006: 3). Discourses on language – *language ideologies* – are among such language uses that shape social order.

Followers of functional approaches to discourse often regard discourses as existing in singular forms (see McHoul, 2001), as with 'the discourse of migration' or 'the discourse of racism'. It is understood that these discourses, as larger bodies of texts and oral statements, delivered by individuals, experts or institutions, bring into being and form the very object they seem to be talking *about*. Thus, discourses are 'practices which systematically form the objects of which they speak' (Foucault, 1973: 74; translation in Cameron, 2001: 15). Accordingly, the specific comprehension of a particular topic arises through speaking and writing about it. As a consequence, social categories like gender, culture, language or ethnicity are not *a priori* givens, but rather are outcomes of discourses. Another crucial aspect is that the existence of discursive categories is dialectically related to positions of power. This means that success in constructing a certain concept as 'true' is always entangled with constructing power and social hierarchies. A foundational aim of analysing discourse is to understand that 'what we assume to be background knowledge or common sense in fact are always ideological representations' (Pennycook, 2001: 81) – namely, the representations of those who have succeeded in disseminating them across wider social spheres.

There are many different discourses. They are interwoven with other discourses and all discourses together, accordingly, are responsible for structuring society. Discourses limit what can be said but at the same time enable particular, historically conditioned ways of understanding the world:

> So, at any given historical conjuncture, it is only possible to write, speak, or think about a given social object (madness, for example) in specific ways and not others. '*A* discourse' would then be whatever constrains – but also enables – writing, speaking, and thinking within such specific historical limits. (McHoul, 2001: 139; italics in original)

Discourse analysis, in this social-constructivist understanding, is not only interested in talk but also encompasses social practice and material artefacts, as the term 'discourse' here 'refers to a broad conglomeration of linguistic and non-linguistic social practices' (Schiffrin *et al.*, 2001: 1). Thus, discourse analysis focuses on the network of statements, objects, structures and acts that contribute to the existence of different fields of knowledge in a given society, which are seen as interrelated to the construction of social hierarchies. It is therefore not only language that is of potential interest but everything that is responsible for the reproduction of a certain concept as true.

The spatial structure of a school classroom is an example of the entanglement of material artefacts and immaterial concepts of meaning. Not only is the teacher allowed to determine the way pupils communicate in the classroom and to decide who can talk. In a traditional classroom, the position of the teacher is co-constructed by the way in which chairs, tables and the blackboard are positioned. Architecture and the organisation of space are here part of the discourse that shapes school life. In order to include such non-verbal parts of discourses, the study of language discourse in transnational salsa communities employs ethnography, as it incorporates the analysis of images, material artefacts and non-verbal behaviour. Yet, although discourses include all types of cultural artefacts, language plays a central role in their constitution. Language is the conveyor of meaning and of ideas about objects, people and things. There is no language-independent concreteness or reality; there is no unmediated access to reality (Bublitz,

2003: 28, 29). A particular focus of the analysis in later chapters is therefore on verbal data, mostly from qualitative interviews.

In analysing interview data, the content and structure of individual verbal utterances are the central focus and these are regarded as indicative of discourses that exist in the wider social sphere. Everything that has meaning and is understandable to others is necessarily linked to broader discourses. It is impossible to make an (understandable) utterance that does not relate to other utterances that have been made before and, thus, the interpretation of individual utterances is simultaneously an analysis of social structures. Bakhtin describes this relationship as follows in an often-quoted passage:

> [A]ny speaker is himself [*sic*] a respondent to a greater or lesser degree. He is not, after all, the first speaker, the one who disturbs the eternal silence of the universe. And he presupposes not only the existence of the language system he is using, but also the existence of preceding utterances – his own and others' – with which his given utterance enters into one kind of relation or another (builds on them, polemicizes them, or simply presumes that they are already known to the listener). Any utterance is a link in a very complexly organized chain of other utterances. (Bakhtin, 1935 [2006]: 101)

The discursive analytic approach 'can be seen as a method for investigating the "social voices" available to the people whose talk analysts collect' (Cameron, 2001: 15). These 'voices', as has been elaborated, do not exist *a priori* but are constructed in social interaction. In this sense, discourse analysis is a post-structuralist theory and method. In contrast to modernist, structuralist approaches to reality, which typically regard categories and structures as 'given' (see e.g. Behrens, 2003; Williams, 1999: 11), post-structuralism conceives that the social world is discursively constructed. It should be noted, however, that this does not mean that structures are conceived of as vague or arbitrary. Despite a general scepticism towards conceptions of truth or supposedly 'natural' social orders, we should be

> reluctant [...] to give up entirely any notion of system and boundary, any notion of constraint (whether physical or social). At the same time, we can no longer see these as fixed, natural, essentialized or objective; rather, we want to understand them as ongoing processes of social construction occurring under specific (and discoverable) conditions (many of them of our making, all of them made sense out of in some way). (Heller, 2007b: 341)

Summarising, discourse constitutes the social world, as it constitutes social structures and the social 'voices' of individuals. Language is the prime means of constructing this world, which is, nevertheless, very structured and 'real'. This also holds true for constructions regarding language. 'A language' is a construct that is interwoven with discourses that have developed in a national age. These conceive the world as 'naturally' divided into different nations with different cultures, territories and languages.

Language Ideology and National Language Discourse

In investigating the 'social voices' available to individuals, language ideologies are a favourable area of research. '[A] definition of language is always, implicitly or explicitly, a definition of human beings in the world' (Williams, 1977: 21). Concepts of language and language use underpin not only linguistic form (as debated in e.g. Silverstein, 1979); notions of the person and the group, of religious ritual, child socialisation, gender relations, the nation-state, schooling and law, and so on, are all interwoven with ideas people have about language (Woolard, 1998: 3). At the same time, '[p]references for particular languages and language varieties are always articulated within the context of an ideology that reflects a society's view of itself' (Romaine, 2007: 685).

> The topic of language ideology is a much-needed bridge between linguistic and social theory, because it relates the microculture of communicative action to political and economic considerations of power and social inequality, confronting macrosocial constraints on language behavior. (Woolard, 1994: 72)

This section first deepens an understanding of discourses on language and their study, and then provides an insight into language ideologies of nationalism, which have had a foundational impact on social and scientific ideas about language in Western contexts.

Language ideologies have been defined as 'shared bodies of commonsense notions about the nature of language in the world' (Rumsey, 1990: 346; see also Heath, 1989; Woolard, 1994, 1998). In emphasising the crucial connections between the realms of the *social* and the *linguistic*, Irvine defines language ideologies as 'the cultural system of ideas about social and linguistic relationships, together with their loading of moral and political interests' (Irvine, 1989: 255). The field of language ideology is broad and encompasses, for example,

> [b]eliefs about how 'language' and 'reality' are related, beliefs about how communication works, and beliefs about linguistic correctness, goodness and badness, articulateness and inarticulateness [...], beliefs about the role of language in a person's identity, beliefs about how languages are learned, and beliefs about what the functions of language should be, who the authorities on language are, whether and how language should be legislated, and so on. (Johnstone, 2008: 66)

In language ideology research, the term *language ideology* encompasses covert indexes of language ideology *in* language and overt discourses *on* language. It is conceived that the 'sitings of ideology' (Woolard, 1998: 9) are, on the one hand, in linguistic practice and, on the other hand, in talk *about* language. There are conscious ideologies but there are also naturalised, unconscious ideologies, and the essence of the study of language ideology is 'to examine the cultural and historical specificity of construals of language' (Woolard, 1998: 8).

The term *ideology* in research on language ideologies is to be differentiated from how it is employed in some other areas of social science. Many social theorists have abandoned working with the concept of *ideology* in favour of the concept of *discourse*, as the term *ideology* may tacitly evoke the idea that there are 'un-ideological' or neutral forms of knowledge. According to Foucauldian discourse theory, however, '"truth" is constituted only within discourses that sustain and are sustained by power' (Woolard, 1998: 7). Differentiating between 'ideological' and 'un-ideological' types of knowledge does not make sense according to this approach. Yet, the term *language ideology*, how it is conceptualised and employed in linguistic anthropology, implies the idea that discourses on language are always interwoven with questions of the social, of power and of power struggles. All notions of language are unavoidably tied to social or political concepts, which is why the distinction between a neutral analysis and a critical analysis of these conceptions is more scalar than dichotomous (Kroskrity, 2000a: 6). The term *language ideology* is very close to the idea of *discourse* as discussed above and will be adopted in the remainder of the present volume, as it is the common term in the tradition to which it owes its existence.

Due to the considerable success of structuralist theories of grammar in the latter part of the 20th century, it was not until the 1990s that the notion of *language ideology* became prominent in linguistics, initially mainly in linguistic anthropology. The reason for this 'late arrival' (Kroskrity, 2000a: 5–7; see also Kroskrity, 2001: 2–4) of the concept of language as a cultural construction is that, for most of the last century, the speaker's linguistic analyses and the non-referential functions of language were neglected areas of study in linguistics.[1] Theoretical trends like post-structuralism and social developments that have put into question modernist, structuralist concepts have contributed to a rising interest in language ideologies since the 1990s. It should be noted that the study of language ideologies does not imply a denial of linguistic structures. A discursive understanding of languages and their structures does not deny their existence and it

> does not mean refuting the essence of syntax or the manner in which language is structured so that the possibilities of meaning are developed. What it does mean is paying attention to the manner in which the infinite possibilities of language are transposed into meaning as the effect of discourse [...]. (Williams, 1999: 5)

Today, the field of research on language ideology is rather elusive. A lot of research is concerned with concepts of language but may use different terms for this (e.g. Doleschal, 2002; Hellinger, 2000; Pavlenko & Piller, 2001); at the same time, there are studies in sociolinguistics and pragmatics that use the term without making reference to the scholarly framework as developed in linguistic anthropology (e.g. Stevenson & Mar-Molinero, 2006a). The different uses of the term, the nomination of similar phenomena with different terms, and the fact that language ideology can be implicit and explicit (see also Woolard, 1998: 9) make a review of the field a complex task. Overall, it is useful to regard language ideology as a 'cluster concept' (Kroskrity, 2001: 5).

Very broadly speaking, there are three different fields of interest in language ideology research (the following categories are an adaptation of Woolard, 1998). Firstly, there is research on *language ideologies and their relationship to linguistic structure* (e.g. Silverstein, 1979). An essential moment in which language ideologies affect linguistic structure is, for example, in language change. The rationalisation of language change that speakers construct is usually based on the idea that language structure should be regular; thus, it is quite common that older structures are given up for the sake of regularity (see also Cameron, 1995, on normative ideologies and their effects on linguistic structure).

Secondly, there is research on *language ideologies in scientific epistemology*. This strand overlaps with language philosophy and discusses the relationship between language, truth and reality (e.g. Joseph & Taylor, 1990). Language ideologies can be observed in any type of science (see several articles on this in Kroskrity, 2000b). Constructions and theories of language that have been developed in linguistics are of particular relevance in this context. They have effects on language ideologies of other sciences, but also on other academic and social discourses. An illustrative example of this is the *family tree model* of languages, which, according to Alter (1999), was drawn on in evolutionary theory and biology, and here co-constructed an evolutionary hierarchy of human cultures. The model of an evolution of languages is thus co-responsible for the construction of cultural hierarchies of 'civilisation', with all their brutal effects under colonialism (see Alter, 1999; Errington, 2008; Irvine, 1995). Research on language ideologies in linguistics is an 'attempt to denaturalize our own intellectual tradition's compartmentalization and reification of communicative social practice' (Woolard, 1998: 9).

Thirdly, there is research on *social discourses about language*. The field is wide and it is probably the one that is primarily associated with the topic of language ideology. The stigmatisation of non-standard languages and of speakers of minority languages is the most commonplace language ideology within the social sphere (see e.g. Lippi-Green, 1997). Linguistic forms are typically ideologised as 'implicating a distinctive kind of people' (Woolard, 1998: 18), which leads to the *meconnaisance*, or misrecognition (Bourdieu, 1980 [2005]), of conceiving of linguistic form as indicative of social, political, intellectual or moral character. In addition to these rather obvious ideologies, there are many tacit ideologies on the nature, functioning or benefit of languages. Examples are the role of written forms of language or of standardised ('correct') language (Romaine, 2007), ideologies related to second language learning, language testing, or relations between language and other discourses, such as neo-liberalism or social cohesion (see e.g. Block *et al*., 2012; Blommaert, 1999; Heller & Duchêne, 2012; Piller, 2001b; Piller & Cho, 2013; Takahashi, 2013).

In Western societies, social discourses about language are usually characterised by the idea that there is an intrinsic relationship between a language and cultural group of people. This concept has been analysed in relation to the development of nationalism and colonialism and it can be referred to as a *national language ideology* (for an elaboration see e.g. Errington, 2008; Hymes, 1968; Rampton, 2000b; Risager, 2006). Communicative practices are understood as materialising in separate language systems, which pertain to the cultural group they 'belong' to and are conceptualised as separate entities, such as *English*, *Spanish* or *German*. This is also referred to as 'language in its differential sense' (as opposed to 'language in its generic sense' – see Bauman, 1999; and also Risager, 2006: 3), and is sometimes written as *Language*, with a capital *L* (Blommaert, 2003; Pennycook, 2004).[2] Although the concept of *Language*, from a lay perspective, may seem simple and straightforward, there have been manifold discussions of its ontology:

> To talk about 'languages' is to assume that there are self-contained sets of syntactic rules and words which exist before and outside of talk, which groups of people share completely, and which everyone in a group accesses and uses in the same way as they talk. But languages in this sense are found only in dictionaries and grammar books, and then incompletely. It could be, in fact, that we think of languages as autonomous and shared precisely because we are used to grammars and dictionaries, because the experiences with language we are most self-conscious about (school experiences, for example) tend to involve the standardized written varieties that are codified in grammars and dictionaries. (Johnstone, 2008: 43–44)

Languages, in their symbolic and in their communicative function, were essential for the national idea right from its beginnings. The postulation that these languages are a precondition for collective identities continues to be relevant for present-day debates on belonging:

> The idea that collective identities and languages are connected in an essentialist way has been a key concept of European modernity; it underlies the formation of the European nation states and it continues to be deeply rooted in our language ideologies. According to this idea, each collectivity (particularly a nation, or a Volk) expresses its own individual character through and in its language. The term 'essentialist' is justified here since it is assumed that there is a 'natural' link between a nation and 'its' language. (Auer, 2007: 2)

Conceptualising language as emerging in separate linguistic systems is thus an effect of conceptualising an intrinsic relationship between collective identity and language: 'the nation-state ideology of language [...] constructed the unit of language through the formation of the nation-state' (Muehlmann & Duchêne, 2007: 105). Considering this, we can say that 'language does not create nationalism, so much as nationalism creates language' (Billig, 1995: 30). National language ideologies are interwoven with a discursive regime that regards the world as divided into separate cultural groups on separate territories. Obviously, this regime is not a 'natural' state of affairs but the result of historical discursive developments.

In investigations of these developments, it has been maintained that 'the acceptance and use by subalterns of a national language and its standardization constituted a critical component of the bourgeoisie establishing hegemony in European states' (Sonntag, 2009: 11; see also Bourdieu, 1980 [2005]). A common code is crucial for the formation of a common identity, above all in 'imagined communities' (Anderson, 1985), as in bourgeois nation-states, in which the *people* form the legitimate political power (on the complementary concept of language in colonial regimes, see Errington, 2008).

Linguistics as an academic discipline developed during the era of the rising power of nation-states. It is therefore not an accident that '[m]odern linguistics itself has been framed and constrained by the one language/one people assumption' (Woolard, 1998: 17; see also Le Page, 1988). Linguistics is thus part of the discourse of power that performs – brings into being – the subject of language (see also Pennycook, 2004). It typically regards *languages* and their boundaries as quasi-'natural' objects of study (see e.g. Cameron, 1995: ch. 1; and the discussion on methodological nationalism in Chapter 1 of the present volume). Yet, boundaries between languages are the result of social differentiation and not of biological processes (an idea that was reified in nationalist 19th-century linguistics – see Errington, 2008: chs 3, 4). In light of the dominance of the nationalist concept of linguistic differentiation, questions about the development of these differentiations were mostly ignored in linguistic studies. We still know little about the ways in which boundaries between languages have been constructed, or about the social processes by which linguistic units become linked to social units (Gal & Irvine, 1995: 970; Gal & Woolard, 1995; Irvine & Gal, 2000; Rampton, 2000b). As Gal and Irvine (1995: 970) argue, these boundaries and social processes 'cannot be understood without a study of the ideas about social and linguistic difference held by socially-positioned speakers'. An analysis of these ideas is the aim of the present study on language ideologies in transnational salsa communities.

Transnationalism, Cosmopolitanism and Sociolinguistics

Through the formation of new, non-national 'imagined communities' (Anderson, 1985), and discourses that transcend national boundaries, the socio-cultural contingency of standardised national languages, pertaining to different national peoples, has become more apparent. A non-national, non-essentialist perspective on language may show

> that language [...] may be serving as a terrain for the construction of boundaries and relations of power in ways that are legitimate within dominant discursive regimes. That constructing language as the problem may serve to mask the construction and reproduction of relations of difference and inequality (since, ostensibly, language can be learned and is

> therefore not inherently exclusionary). That learning (and abandoning) languages may be a matter of social positioning, with all the risks and dangers (and thrills and opportunities) that entails. That operating with the idea of language as bounded in the first place may be primarily a matter of reproducing specific discursive regimes. (Heller, 2007b: 345)

In contrast to conceptualising language as 'little more than a product/output generated by semantic, grammatical and phonological systems, which are themselves regarded as either mental structures or as sets of social conventions' (Rampton, 2006: 16), language may be approached as an effect of social practices that produce 'specific discursive regimes'. Studying language ideologies in transnational contexts means to get a glimpse of the discursive regimes beyond nationalism that are operating in contemporary, globalised societies, and how these may have an impact on concepts of language.

A 'practice'-oriented view on language has existed in linguistics for a long time, particularly in anthropological and ethnographic approaches (see e.g. Gumperz & Hymes, 1964). Globalisation and transnationalism, and the theories that have been created on the grounds of these cultural developments, have led to a new popularity of linguistic research in this vein. In this section, I briefly introduce the notion of *transnationalism*, and the related term *cosmopolitanism*, as developed in sociology and cultural anthropology, as these are valuable for overcoming methodological nationalism in linguistics. I secondly present a short chronological overview of studies that have developed non-national outlooks on language and that were a foundational inspiration for the study presented in subsequent chapters.

The terms *transnationalism* and *globalisation* are sometimes used interchangeably and it can be difficult to differentiate the two. The term *globalisation* is used widely in popular discourses. In sociology, it has been described as 'the intensification of worldwide social relations which link distant localities in such a way that local happenings are shaped by events occurring many miles away and vice versa' (Giddens, 1990: 15; for other definitions of globalisation, see also Appadurai, 1996; Beck, 1997; Castells, 2002; Hall, 1994; Papastergiadis, 2000; Pries, 2001; Robertson, 1992). *Transnationalism* is a less-used term that is found in postcolonial discourse (e.g. Gilroy, 1987; Said, 1978), cultural anthropology and sociology (Glick Schiller *et al.*, 1997; Pries, 2008). In these contexts, the term describes one aspect of globalisation, namely social interactions and social relations that transcend national boundaries. In the context of sociological and anthropological studies, studies on the settling practices of migrants were crucial in establishing a more transcending gaze on culture (see Glick Schiller *et al.*, 1997; Pries, 1997). These brought to light that migration is not simply a one-way process that ends with the migrant settling in a 'given' and stable culture. Migrants do not necessarily attempt to completely 'integrate' into a host society but maintain close ties with their home countries, develop transnational social networks and construct new identity positions. This realisation not only questions concepts of 'assimilation' or the 'integration' of migrants. It calls into question the theoretical framing of apparently 'given' cultures, as migration processes, in their ability to impact on 'host' societies, make it apparent that all cultures are the outcome of historical social struggles over cultural difference and power.

The recognition of the constructedness of national cultures was followed by a surge of theories based on the idea of the 'trans'. The prefix *trans-* relates to concepts, people or products in-between, to third spaces, to hybrid forms of reality and identity (for different versions of the concept, see e.g. Anzaldúa, 1987; Bhabha, 1994; Ong, 1999: 4; for a discussion of theoretical backgrounds of transgressive theories, see Pennycook, 2007: 36–40). A focus on the state of in-between shows that all cultures are, in effect, the result of mixing and borrowing. Notions that make use of the prefix *trans-* thus

> refer not merely to the spread of particular forms of culture across boundaries, nor only to the existence of supercultural commonalities (cultural forms that transcend locality). They draw our attention instead to the constant processes of borrowing, bending and blending of cultures, to the communicative practices of people interacting across different linguistic and communicative codes, borrowing, bending and blending languages into new modes of expression. (Pennycook, 2007: 47)

Although the 'constant processes of borrowing, bending and blending of cultures' can be found in any cultural realm, they become more apparent if people participate in cultural activities that are traditionally considered to relate to places elsewhere. Cultural practices like salsa dancing in Australia or Germany, while not necessarily based on individual migration trajectories, create 'forms of community consciousness and solidarity that maintain identifications outside the national time/space' (Clifford, 1994: 308). Communities constituted on the basis of cultural flows that have made music, dance and other practices travel are therefore forms of transnationalism that have the potential to destabilise national accounts of culture. The fact that in today's Sydney or Frankfurt, Latin American salsa is more popular than German polka or Australian bush dance shows the degree of transnational blending that shapes contemporary societies.

A concept related to transnationalism is *cosmopolitanism*. I here focus on the concept as discussed in the 1990s in cultural anthropology (see Hannerz, 1996b), which analyses the effects of transnational cultural contact on individual positioning with regard to the culture of origin and 'other' cultures. Hannerz's idea of *cosmopolitans* makes visible the hierarchy potential of transnational interactions. As contact with an 'other' language and its functions in constructing class identity are central in salsa communities, the concept, despite theoretical difficulties, is useful in interpreting empirical discursive data. According to Ulf Hannerz, cosmopolitan people have

> first of all an orientation, a willingness to engage with the Other. [This] entails an intellectual and esthetic openness toward divergent cultural experiences, a search for contrasts rather than uniformity. (Hannerz, 1996a: 103)

A cosmopolitan person is someone who wants to become competent in 'other' semiotic systems. One effect of an engagement with alien systems of meaning is that '[o]ne's understandings have expanded, a little more of the world is somehow under control' (Hannerz, 1996a: 103). Additionally, this understanding results in a changed relationship to the culture of origin. For the cosmopolitan, contact and cultural competence in another culture 'implies personal autonomy *vis-á-vis* the culture where he [*sic*] originated. He has his obvious competence with regard to it, but he can choose to disengage from it' (Hannerz, 1996a: 104). Thus, cosmopolitans develop a form of cultural meta-knowledge, which enables them to relativise systems of meaning of origin. The development of meta-knowledge and the ability to construct a non-naturalised relationship to heritage cultures is crucial here. Meta-cultural competence and knowledge are increasingly vital, in the globalised job market for instance, as well as in indexing cultural capital (Bourdieu, 1979). Therefore, Hannerz conceives of cosmopolitans as '"the new class", people with credentials, decontextualized cultural capital' (Hannerz, 1996a: 109).

At the same time, the cosmopolitan is dependent on the existence of local, non-cosmopolitan structures. Acquiring local forms of knowledge is a precondition to becoming cosmopolitan; thus, 'there can be no cosmopolitans without locals' (Hannerz, 1996a: 111). This understanding of cosmopolitanism relies on cultural essentialisms, and is therefore theoretically problematic; yet, Hannerz's *cosmopolitanism* mirrors cultural concepts documented in this study. Another critical point are the class divisions Hannerz makes in assuming that 'intellectuals' are prototypical cosmopolitans, while he devalues the cultural competence of, for example, labour migrants or illegalised people. Thus, Hannerz has been criticised for his elitist view on cosmopolitans (Römhild, 2007). *Cosmopolitanism*, in this understanding, seems to be outdated and problematic for its class bias and essentialisms. Yet, it cannot be ignored that empirical data are never free from problematic, class-biased and essentialist assumptions. Furthermore,

> [w]hat often seems to be overlooked in discussions of local, global and hybrid relations is the way in which the local may involve not only the take up of the global, or a localised form of cosmopolitanism, but also may equally be about the take up of local forms of static and monolithic identity and culture. (Otsuji & Pennycook, 2009: 4–5)

Overall, considering the existence of transnational discourses and of cosmopolitan forms of identity, it can be maintained that simplified ethnic or national frames of reference are no longer (or maybe have never been) sufficient for an understanding of social processes and cultural meaning systems. Language is an essential tool in the creation of such meaning systems. However, as discussed above, due to the 'birth' of linguistics as a science in 19th-century national contexts (Woolard, 1998: 17) and the popularity of structuralism in 20th-century linguistics, transnational theories have entered the field of linguistics relatively late. Contemporary scholars who deconstruct the idea of language as a 'given' system have become prominent within the last two decades (e.g. Auer, 1999; Bauman & Briggs, 2003; Blommaert, 2003; Cameron, 1995; Gal & Irvine, 1995; Heller, 2007a; Irvine, 2001; Makoni & Pennycook, 2007; Pennycook, 2004; Rampton, 2000b; Silverstein, 2000). The problematisation of the 'language–culture–nation ideological nexus' (Heller, 2007a: 7), which relates to theories of the *trans-*, now has become popular, especially in sociolinguistics, linguistic anthropology and related disciplines. The newest trend in this context is the debate on *superdiversity*, which pleas for a methodological and theoretical paradigm shift in order to account for the increased social and cultural diversity. This also involves a de-essentialised view of language and calls for ethnographic studies in linguistics (see below and e.g. Arnaut, 2012; Blommaert & Rampton, 2011).

There are, however, much older accounts of non-essentialist views on language. Dell Hymes, a renowned linguistic anthropologist whose first seminal works appeared during the 1960s, dealt with the problematic theoretical foundations anthropologists and linguists have with regard to language. In the following quote, he calls 'Herderian' the idea that a people and a language have an intrinsic connection and considers it an 'inferior sort of fairy tale':

> Most usual anthropological statements about language are an inferior sort of fairy tale, spun from an unexamined assumption of the sort I have called 'Herderian'. We need to build a theory of language that starts from what we can see to be actually the case in the world, man's polymorphous (and to the ethnologist perhaps perverse) capacity to communicate in codes other than language, to use more languages than one, to make shifting choices as to codes and communication over time. (Hymes, 1968: 42)

During the 1980s, a linguistic anthropological study on Belizean Creole was the most prominent publication to overcome a methodologically nationalist view on the existence of 'languages'. In their empirical research conducted from the 1950s through to the 1970s, Robert B. Le Page and Andrée Tabouret-Keller observed the 'birth' of Belizean Creole and analysed the discourses that bring a 'language' into being (Le Page & Tabouret-Keller, 1985). Ahead of the advent of post-structural theory in linguistics, they created a comprehensive theory on the discursive evolution of linguistic categories. 'Languages' are here demonstrated to be an effect of social discourses, dialectically related to the (ethnic) groups that speak them.

Another 1980s contribution that helped establish the concept of the discursive evolution of 'language' is an article chapter entitled 'Linguistic Utopias', by Mary Louise Pratt, in which she criticises most of 20th-century linguistics as a utopian science of a 'linguistics of community' (Pratt, 1987: 49) and envisages a linguistics

> that place[s] at its centre the operation of language *across* lines of social differentiation, a linguistics that focuse[s] on modes and zones of contact between dominant and dominated groups, between persons of different and multiple identities, speakers of different languages, that focuse[s] on how such speakers constitute each other relationally and in difference, how they enact differences in language. (Pratt, 1987: 60)

A more recent theoretical–methodological framework that overcomes simplified notions of the language–culture nexus, and that creates a linguistics that focuses on 'the operation of language across lines of social differentiation', was developed in Rampton's work on *crossing* (Rampton, 1995a). The term *language crossing* quickly became part of the terminological repertoire to describe language practices in multilingual environments. Based on empirical research in multi-ethnic, multilingual classrooms, Rampton's work is one of the starting points of what can be considered transnational sociolinguistics. In his study, teenagers of different ethnic descent (mainly Anglo, Asian and West Indian) used (Caribbean-derived) Creole, Panjabi and stylised Asian English, and the semantic-referential competence of the 'crossers' – speakers who have no native competence in the respective languages – was very limited and often confined to greeting formulae or terms of insult or enthusiasm. Different languages were used for different purposes and had different symbolic meanings. Crossing into Creole, for example, was usually associated with youth culture and joking, while stylised Asian English was, rather, related to ethnic and generational stereotypes (see also Rampton, 1995b). The notion of crossing thus

> focuses on code alternation by people who are not accepted members of the group associated with the second language they employ. It is concerned with switching into languages that are not generally thought to belong to you. This kind of switching, in which there is a distinct sense of movement across social and ethnic boundaries, raises issues of social legitimacy that participants need to negotiate, and that analysts could usefully devote more attention to. (Rampton, 1995a: 280)

Crossing deconstructs the notion of *language* in practical terms, as it challenges 'ethnic absolutism' (Rampton, 1995a: 317) in denaturalising the link between language and ethnic identity. Rampton's work also shows that languages have wider social meanings and that 'social knowledge about ethnicity is actively processed in informal interaction' (Rampton, 1995a: 283). This can also be observed in salsa communities, where, for example, ethnic stereotypes of Latin culture have an impact on language ideologies, often leading to salsa dancers learning Spanish or associating Spanish with non-capitalist values.

Crossing is generally rather common (see Rampton, 1995a: 280–289, which also includes a discussion of the difference between code-switching and crossing) and, as identities are performed that do not fit into a national paradigm, deconstructs national language ideologies. It becomes visible in this approach that communities and 'their' languages are forms of semiotic signs. They are relevant for constructing social boundaries and these are not necessarily based only on ethnic difference. They can also be based on 'objects of desire, fashion accoutrements and/or marketised life-style options, with "authenticity" becoming as much an issue of commodity branding as a matter of ethnic roots' (Rampton, 2000b: 10). We will consider similar observations in later chapters.

Another contemporary scholar closely associated with the questioning of an essentialist concept of language is Alastair Pennycook (see e.g. Pennycook,

2003, 2004; also Makoni & Pennycook, 2007). Based on a profound concern with colonial discourse (Pennycook, 1998), his writings bring to the fore the constructed nature of languages. According to Pennycook, the discursive construct of language comes into being through discourse itself: 'languages are not so much entities that pre-exist our linguistic performances as the sedimented products of repeated acts of identity' (Pennycook, 2007: 13). The constant repetition of language form in interaction brings into being what is commonly understood as *language* (see also the related argument in Hopper, 1988). Furthermore, '[l]anguages, as described by linguistics and applied linguistics, are inventions of the disciplines that make them' (Pennycook, 2010: 129). Pennycook's argumentation is in this respect similar to the post-structuralist concepts of Foucault (see Chapter 2).

Languages as inventions, however, have a cognitive reality for the speakers who use them. The aim of studying language ideologies in transnational contexts is not primarily to show that languages are discursive constructs but to document the discourses that influence their construction and conception. In order to do this, the interrelationships of discourses, constructions and values have to be mapped. Jan Blommaert's *The Sociolinguistics of Globalization* is constructive in this sense and has been influential in the interpretation of empirical data in this study.

Published in 2010, Blommaert's *The Sociolinguistics of Globalization* develops an analytical framework that allows for non-national perspectives and for the inclusion of micro- and macro-discourses that contribute to the symbolic functions of languages in particular contexts. A central point in Blommaert's considerations is the fact that, although linguistic items acquire meaning in micro-situations, influenced by the conventions that exist within a particular speech community, they are at the same time related to systems of meaning elsewhere, beyond the communities, systems that potentially are transnational. In an age of globalisation, it is thus different sociolinguistic systems that interact in constructing linguistic meaning in local contexts. Therefore,

> [s]ociolinguistics in the age of globalization needs to look way beyond the speech community, to sociolinguistic systems and how they connect and relate to one another. Big things matter if we want to understand the small things of discourse. (Blommaert, 2010: 41)

Blommaert (citing Lefebvre) uses the term *scale* to conceptualise the relationship between different sociolinguistic systems. Scales are '"levels" or "dimensions" (Lefebvre 2003: 136–150) at which particular forms of normativity, patterns of language use and expectations are thereof organized' (Blommaert, 2010: 36). There are local (micro-)scales and global (macro-)scales and intermediate scales (for example, the state level) and '[e]very human interaction develops situationally, at a microscopic scale of social structure. Yet, it is always embedded in larger patterns – linguistic, social, cultural, historical – and draws meaning from these larger patterns' (Blommaert *et al.*, 2005: 204). Higher-level scales contrast with lower-level scales. Higher-level scales typically have a wider reach and are perceived to be more 'central' than lower-level scales. By analysing language use and discourses on language, it can be observed that 'spaces are ordered and organized in relation to one another, stratified and layered, with processes belonging to one scale entering processes at another scale' (Blommaert *et al.*, 2005: 203).

If, for example, interaction takes place in a certain language variety, then this is a higher-level (e.g. regional or national) influence on an otherwise strictly situational event (Blommaert *et al.*, 2005: 204). Higher-level scales are 'contexts that influence language long before it is produced in the form of utterances' (Blommaert, 2005: 77). The usage of Spanish in Sydney's or Frankfurt's salsa contexts is an effect of a higher-level – non-national – scale on a particular situation, where the transnational scale interacts with the local scale of community norms. Overall, a crucial point in analysing transnational language ideology is therefore the fact that local, regional, national and global scales are interrelated:

> Though the various scales operate with some degree of autonomy and according to rules largely internal to them, the different scales are interlocked. State-level activities, for instance, such as policies in education, are responsive both to influences from higher-level, transnational scales (consider the growing concern with English in almost every education system in the world) as well as from lower-level, intra-national scales (the national and regional political dynamics, minority issues...). Hierarchical relations between scales are unpredictable: when there is a conflict between local and transnational (globalization) pressures on a government, for instance, it is by no means sure that the transnational influences will prevail. But the point is: scales are not neutral items, they attribute meaning, value, structure and characteristics to the processes that they are part of. (Blommaert *et al.*, 2005: 202)

Overall, the notion of *scale* is a vertical metaphor of space that not only captures the fact that there is a relationship between language norms and concepts of space, but that also maps social hierarchies and the different weight of different discourses in a hierarchical and spatial pattern. As indicated in the quote above, the spatial hierarchy of the local, national and global dimension does not necessarily mean that the global scale is the most influential scale in a given situation. By foregrounding the multi-layered nature of contemporary sociolinguistic economies, this theoretical notion is constructive in analysing the processes at work in language ideologies in transnational salsa communities. A *scale*, however, can also be understood as a form of discourse, in the Foucauldian understanding of the term (see Chapter 2). Thus, in the remainder of this book, the term *discourse* prevails in referring to the systems of meanings that potentially contribute to language ideologies.

In Blommaert's framework, different *scales* relate to different *indexical orders*. An indexical order is 'the metapragmatic organizing principle behind what is widely understood as the "pragmatics" of language' (Blommaert, 2010: 37). The indexical order produces social categories (and is in this sense also very close to the term 'discourse' as introduced above) and indexical orders are themselves ordered in a hierarchical fashion, depending on the scales they relate to. In a globalised world, different orders of indexicality come into contact. It is thus important to note that a semiotic sign, for example an accent, can have different meanings in different indexical orders. The functions of semiotic signs (linguistic varieties, accents, particular linguistic features, etc.) cannot be presupposed but have to be interpreted in a way that relates to a particular order of indexicality, which is, however, not necessarily the same for all participants in an interaction, so that misinterpretations can occur. 'Whenever discourses travel across the globe, what is carried with them is their shape, but their value, meaning, or function do not often travel along' (Blommaert, 2005: 72). We will see instances of this phenomenon in later chapters.

As mentioned above, the most recent debate in the linguistic study of transnational contexts is the one on *superdiversity* (Blommaert & Rampton, 2011; Vertovec, 2007). The term originally stems from sociological and anthropological contexts to denote 'the increase in the categories of migrants, not only in terms of nationality, ethnicity, language, and religion, but also in terms of motives, patterns and itineraries of migration' (Blommaert & Rampton, 2011: 1; see also Vertovec, 2010). In the context of sociolinguistics, the term relates to the observation that ethnic categories are no longer sufficient to make sense of linguistic practices in superdiverse urban contexts and is therefore now associated with an understanding that

> named languages have now been denaturalised, the linguistic is treated as just one semiotic among many, inequality and innovation are positioned together in a dynamics of pervasive normativity, and the

contexts in which people orient their interactions reach far beyond the communicative event itself. (Blommaert & Rampton, 2011: 1)

Thus, the study presented in the following chapters can be understood as a study of the sociolinguistics of superdiversity in its attempt to analyse language discourse as one semiotic among many in which individuals orient their interactions beyond the communicative events they take part in.

To summarise this chapter, we have seen that discourse shapes the social world, which is the basic theoretical tenet of studying transnational language ideologies. We have also seen that discourses on language are among these socially constructive discourses. National discourse has a foundational impact on discourses on language, on societal discourses, and also on conceptions of language in linguistics. Finally, the idea has been posited that developments of globalisation and transnationalisation have brought about a new interest in questioning linguistic axioms that are based on national discourse. Some approaches working in this vein have been introduced that are particularly relevant for this study. Before I analyse empirical data from the respective communities, the following chapter will give a brief account of the overall cultural context in which these communities are based: salsa.

Notes

(1) However, 'many of the formative movements of early linguistics – the Prague School, American and European Structuralism, Russian Formalism, and others' – considered culturally and socially contingent 'meta-language' a crucial component of verbal communication (Coupland & Jaworski, 2004: 17).

(2) Note that this is different in generative syntax, where *L*anguage means the overall capacity of humans to speak (see Carnie, 2013: ch. 1).

3 Transnational Salsa – Cultural Reinventions of the Global in Local Contexts

This chapter provides background knowledge about salsa – the history of salsa as well as some general aspects of the contemporary cultural practice of salsa in global contexts. A full understanding of the interpretation of empirical data requires some knowledge of the development of salsa and of the cultural discourses that exist within salsa. The discussion here stems from academic texts on the one hand, and on my experiences as a participant observer on the other. I first give historical insights into the development of salsa dance and music; secondly, I present some notes on Western salsa as a case of cultural reinvention in global, transnational contexts. This reinvention typically involves heteronormative ideologies with regard to gender, as discussed. Additionally, before turning to the empirical data of the respective communities in Chapters 4–6, it is crucial that different salsa dance styles are linked to different social and cultural ideologies. This is subject of the final section of this chapter.

A Short History of Salsa

A Western gaze on salsa conceptualises it as somehow 'Latin' and often produces a monolithic and thus monocultural perspective on salsa as 'exotic' and 'other'. In printed media relating to salsa, this typically involves images of people with dark hair or skin, palm trees, sunshine, certain gender ideologies, particular hair and clothing styles, and the like. All of my informants consider salsa to be related to the Spanish-speaking world, but many salsa 'aficionados', including professional dancers, have no accurate knowledge of the origins of salsa. Some see it as related to Spain (from where it does not originate) or to Cuba (from where most of its predecessors stem, but that is only half the story), while others vaguely call it a 'Latin' dance. The cultural history of salsa is complex and confirms Lipsitz's observation that 'today's contemporary popular music retains residual contradictions of centuries of colonialism, class domination, and racism' (Lipsitz, 1994: 5). As salsa's history is one reason for today's divisions in local salsa scenes, it is important to have a basic grasp of it; furthermore, it is important to overcome simplified notions of salsa, as often exist in non-Latin contexts. The following account is overall based on Pietrobruno, whose book gives a more comprehensive and precise introduction to salsa (Pietrobruno, 2006: especially ch. 1).

The history of salsa transcends national boundaries, within and outside of the Americas. In salsa, transnational connections are not new. In the Caribbean, where forerunners of salsa stem from, and in postcolonial environments in general, it is particularly obvious that relationships between location and culture often do not fit into a national paradigm. Discourses related to different geographical levels have here been interacting for a long time. Thus, without the slave trade and the colonial exploitation of Africans in the Americas, salsa as it exists now would not have developed. Salsa is based on a number of African and European dances that, beginning in the 18th century, were fused in colonial Caribbean contexts. Salsa has several forerunners, among them *son* and *danzon*, both fusions of European and African dance and music styles, which developed during the 19th century in Cuba. In the 20th century, *mambo*, the *chachachá* and elements of *rock'n'roll* furthermore contributed to the emergence of salsa (for a more detailed overview, see Pietrobruno, 2006). Salsa was transnational right from its beginnings, as the fusion of Afro-Cuban culture with European practices was always a crucial element. The creation of the Caribbean as a transnational space is linked to these hybrid music cultures, where sailors 'served as an informal but vital link in the diffusion of [...] salsa recordings' (Waxer, 2002b: 13 see also Waxer, 2002a). Diverse transnational musical ties across the Caribbean – as also with reggae or dance-hall music – remain alive today.

There are heated debates on the first use of the word *salsa* and where salsa originally stems from (see different opinions e.g. in Aparicio, 1998; Pietrobruno, 2006; and in the large number of internet resources on the topic). Some say that Venezuela is the birthplace of salsa, as the term was spread after the release of the record *Llegó la Salsa* by Frederico y su combo latino in Caracas in 1964 (Waxer, 2002a: 219). Yet, despite this, both the vibrant music scene of New York, where diverse music and styles mingled, and the special circumstances of the Puerto Rican diaspora in New York (see below) were decisive elements in the creation of salsa. Ultimately, due to its transnational and intrinsically hybrid nature, it does not really make sense to discuss the 'real' origin of salsa. 'Although the Puerto Rico–New York–Cuba nexus remains a central axis for the creation and commercial production of salsa' (Waxer, 2002b: 6), salsa presents a vital case of the 'translocation' of culture, the emergence of a community from among different localities of production and reception (Santos Febres, 1997; quoted in Waxer, 2002b: 5).

For contemporary salsa, two historical events have to be regarded as crucial. One is the Jones Act of 1917, which granted US citizenship to Puerto Ricans, after the US had invaded Puerto Rico in 1898 (Picó, 1986). This caused the migration of a large number of Puerto Ricans to New York, who brought along the already fused forms of Caribbean dance and music. The second event is the Cuban Revolution in 1959 (Perez-Stable, 1998). The isolation of communist Cuba, which hitherto had been dominant in the production of music, and the Puerto Rican population in the US 'would eventually provide a creative space for Latinos [*sic*] within the United States to develop U.S.-based dance' (Pietrobruno, 2006: 49) and this space, with its transnational ties, was responsible for the birth of salsa.

While there are most certainly multiple 'first' appearances, salsa appeared in the mid-1960s in New York and not only fused European and African elements but was actually a blending of Cuban dance music with jazz styles, as Hispanics, Afro-Americans and others met in New York music clubs and dance halls (see Pietrobruno, 2006: 48; Waxer, 2002b: 4) – popular music here shows its avant-garde status in overcoming ethnic boundaries. Salsa's arrival in the 1960s, however, was not only based on cultural contact but was also linked to political aims. Hispanics in the US, inspired by the Black Panthers (Ogbar, 2004), started to advocate Latino/Latina pride to fight racism and to foster cultural consciousness of Latin Americans (Manuel, 1995: 73). 'Born as an expression of Puerto Rican self-awareness and New York Latino [*sic*] pride' (Pietrobruno, 2006: 54), salsa had a strong political message in its beginnings. Violence on the streets, ghetto life, experiences of inequality, American imperialism and memories of a lost home are thus topics of many of the early salsa tracks (see also Waxer, 2002b: 4):

> From the 1970s on salsa became a revolutionary music in New York, Puerto Rico, Venezuela, Colombia and many Latin cities, reaching the peak of its social change manifesto in 1978, with Rubén Blades and Willie Colón's best-selling salsa album *Siembra*. (Berríos-Miranda, 2002: 24)

That album was indeed a focal point of the 1970s salsa movement and many of its lyrics are decidedly political in content. A famous example is the song 'La chica de plástica' (Box 3.1), which illustrates the political positioning of early salsa.

The song, in the context of a Latin diaspora in New York, criticises US American middle-class values for focusing on superficial material success

Box 3.1 'La chica de plástica'

Rubén Blades and Willie Colón

Ella era una chica plástica de esas que veo por ahi
She was one of those plastic girls that I see around here

De esas que cuando se agitan sudan chanel number three
One of those who sweat Chanel number three when they move

[...]

Oye latino oye hermano oye amigo
Listen Latino, listen brother, listen friend

Nunca vendas tu destino por el oro ni la comodidad
Never sell your destiny for money or for convenience

[...]

only. At the same time, the song appeals to a Latin community, who are supposed to strive for non-materialistic values. The binary construction of North Americans as materialistic, who are contrasted with the inhabitants of South America, who, instead, value their community and *el corazón* (the heart), is a very common and still salient construction in Latin America. It has been a central topic in Latin American literary discourses since the 19th century, where the modernist text *Ariel* takes a prominent place (Rodó, 1900; Rodríguez Monegal, 1980). The concept has been influential in the formation of Latin American identity and the song 'La chica de plástica' reconstructs it. A binary opposition of US Americans (*gringos*) as capitalist and Latin Americans as adhering to 'true', often decidedly left-wing values is still highly visible in contemporary Latin American political discourse today. In the analysis of contemporary salsa communities in Chapters 4–6, this binary opposition will reappear, albeit appropriated differently according to the local and national contexts.

Since the 1980s, the political background of salsa has become almost completely invisible:

> The salsa that has been popular since the late 1970s differs significantly from the music that reigned during the explosive years of the 1960s

> and 1970s. Concern with the working-class conditions of barrio life and the issue of Latin solidarity, related to Fania[1]-produced salsa, has been replaced by sentimental love lyrics. Salsa has lost its political edge. (Pietrobruno, 2006: 56)

The issues that had moved Latinos and Latinas in the 1970s were no longer as prevalent and were now associated with an older generation. Not only did the political contents of salsa songs disappear during the 1980s, but the whole salsa movement shrunk during that time (Waxer, 2002b).

In the 1990s, a renewed success of salsa was linked to the realisation that people of Latin descent had developed substantial buying power on the US market. Before that, the Hispanic population had been considered too poor to make it worthwhile to target them with advertising (Farley, 1999). The growing number and buying power of US Latinas and Latinos (Waxer, 2002b: 9) led to a rise of advertising in Spanish and thus the number of radio channels in Spanish grew – as did the opportunity to produce and sell Latin-based music in Spanish. Despite its political history, the new context of the 1990s productions had moved away from Latin culture signifying barrio life; salsa was now promoted as romantic but lively dance music for a mainly Latin audience and was accordingly called *salsa romántica*.

As Frances Aparicio has noted, the more commercialised version of salsa music meant not only a loss of political meaning but was also a move away from the very masculine discourses of more traditional salsa, in which *machismo* models produced passive images of women (Aparicio, 2002). Newer types of salsa music, in contrast, opened up a cultural space for women musicians and all-women bands. Thus, the more commercialised versions of salsa from the 1990s were less oppressive in terms of gender discrimination and traditionally gendered identity. Furthermore, newer salsa in the US has developed into a hybrid genre and is often interwoven with *reggaetón*, hip-hop, RnB and house music, and 'allows young Latino/as to reaffirm their own national identities and simultaneously to move across cultural, racial, musical, and linguistic boundaries' (Aparicio, 2002: 143). The movement of salsa towards contemporary hybrid genres, interestingly, seems to be mainly confined to the transnational spaces of origin of salsa, while salsa in non-Latin ('white') contexts is, as has been mentioned, typically seen as a rather monolithic, traditional activity. A 'white' folkloristic gaze on Caribbean dance culture as somehow 'Latin', 'traditional', 'exotic' and 'romantic', as we will see, can cause some Latin Americans to avoid salsa contexts.

It is also important to note that in many Latin American contexts, salsa has class connotations (Aparicio, 1998; this is also reported in my interviews). This is linked to the racial background of salsa. The origins of Cuban music and dance are partly based in African traditions that were brought to the Caribbean with the slave trade (Alén, 1984). The rhythms of Cuban music and also many dance moves that are taught in salsa classes today can be traced back to African traditions (Pietrobruno, 2006: ch. 1). As discrimination against African-derived cultures and people persists, the African elements of salsa add to its lower status in many Latin American countries, where European-derived music styles have a higher prestige. A lot of younger Latin Americans in Latin America prefer rock and pop music, as salsa links not only to the traditional culture of their parents but also to lower-class status. Of course, there are places where salsa *is* part of the local youth culture, for example in Colombia. In many countries of Latin America, however, for example Chile or Argentine, salsa has no tradition at all and salsa parties here appeared only after the dance had become famous in Europe and the US.

In North American white middle-class contexts, salsa became famous during the 1990s, and this influenced the distribution of salsa to a worldwide audience, including Latin American contexts, where salsa formerly had signified a music for the poor and coloured. In many places all around the world, salsa is now understood to be a Latin-derived music and dance, with its songs predominantly in Spanish, whose audience is Latin Americans, their descendants, or white people with an interest in Latin music. In comparison with hip-hop, rock or pop, salsa has not completely melted into Western mainstream music markets. It is still linked to an 'ethnic' (Latin) background but has found a niche within Western white mainstream music culture.

Reinventing Salsa in the Western World

At the beginning of the 21st century, salsa has become a truly global phenomenon, 'with audiences and practitioners ranging from Tokyo to Dakar' (Waxer, 2002b: 3). Salsa is distributed all over the world, adopted, adapted, appropriated and enjoyed by people from very diverse backgrounds and thus means very different things in different contexts. Yet, there seem to be some general features of salsa culture that are common in many Western countries. Thus, first of all, salsa communities in contexts like Frankfurt or Sydney are typically not reproducing heritage culture of Latin people in a traditional way but develop out of a mix of Western[2] imaginations and desires regarding 'Latinness', and Latin American migrants' (or their descendants') negotiations of identity in contexts of diaspora.

Latin Americans, on the one hand, often become passionate about salsa and develop a 'Latin' identity only when they reside in non-Latin American countries; this is related to a need to reinvent cultural origins or construct ties of ethnic solidarity. Latin migrants, irrespective of location or class background, share similar experiences. 'At home', in Latin American countries, divisions between different nations are often emphasised; a 'Latin' identity is usually not part of an everyday identity repertoire. In migrant contexts, a common history and language, related cultural features and the experience of being approached as 'Latin' or 'Latino' and 'Latina'[3] cause some Latin Americans to adopt a pan-Latin consciousness. Interest in salsa is very often related to the development of such a 'Latin' identity, which I also observed in Sydney and Frankfurt (for similar observations, see Aparicio & Jáquez, 2003, for the US; Papadopoulos, 2003, for Germany; Pietrobruno, 2006, for Canada; Román-Velázquez, 2002, for the UK). In this sense, people of Latin American descent who perform salsa as part of their heritage culture often create a form of imagined cultural nostalgia (see Appadurai, 1998: 18, 19).

It is therefore common but nevertheless wrong to approach people of Latin American descent as necessarily legitimate and 'authentic' salsa dancers. It can be difficult to draw a line between 'real' Latinos/Latinas and others. Typically, ethnic difference is constructed on the basis of the heritage of parents or grandparents. Salsa teachers from Latin American countries often learn salsa wherever their migration trajectory has brought them. Yet, it must not be forgotten that some people of Latin descent do dance salsa as part of their ethnic heritage and have learned it as children. In my sample, the latter were people of Colombian descent, while I met several people with Chilean or Mexican background who had learned salsa in Germany or Australia. At the same time, all 'genuine' Cuban dance teachers (first-generation migrants) that I met during the research had been educated in classical dance in Cuba and were not actually trained salsa dancers. As their expertise in European dance was not appreciated in Europe or Australia, they were more successful in selling what a racially stratified market expected from non-white people. This ties in with the observation of Western audiences typically constructing monolithic and partly stereotyped images of Latin 'others' and their culture.

For Europeans, Australians and other Westerners, on the other hand, salsa can be 'a gateway to the cultural Other, a fascinating and often exotic world where new selves find liberation from cultural strictures' (Waxer, 2002b: 3). Non-Latin individuals become part of a 'Latin' cultural space through the activity of salsa dancing, which is often described as a highly positive experience. Discovering oneself as a 'lively', warm-hearted, and emotional person of integrity is here central, which is set in contrast to the otherwise dominant demand to be professional and to be 'cool' (see Chapter 4, for example). Creating hyper-masculine and hyper-feminine identities seems to be part of the parcel of this 'liberation from cultural strictures' (see below on gender).

On the basis of participant observation, I can relate to the experience of 'liberation' in salsa. Learning to dance salsa also for me meant to find a 'new self', different from my professional identity and partly liberated from the dogma of 'cool' that predominates in many other contemporary music and nightlife cultures. When I started research, I had several years of experience in working in a house and electro club. I found the atmosphere in salsa parties liberating in that I did not feel obliged to perform a 'cool', unimpressed know-all. Smiling and not knowing how to dance is okay in salsa parties and I would always find someone who showed me how to dance when I was new. I also knew that most of my house club friends would find salsa dancing pretty uncool, almost embarrassing. As I perceived the way interaction takes place between strangers as unusually open for a German context (where I started to conduct fieldwork), I assume that the friendly and non-exclusive attitude in salsa events partly relates to an imaginative reproduction of 'Latin' ways of interaction (which may in part also be based on actual experiences that dancers, including myself, have had in Latin America).

Next to the imaginative sphere of an 'exoticised other' that is responsible for the dance's popularity, the very physical experience that is made possible through dancing also has to be taken into account in understanding Western salsa. Bodily interaction is a vital aspect of salsa events. Tangible human bodies and the relatively fixed rules of the dance steps form an interesting contrast to the performance of an 'other' identity in an imagined space of longing. The attractiveness of the physical side of salsa (corporeal contact) and of its fixed rules and roles might also be understood as a counter-culture to virtual and fluid forms of relationship as they exist in online networks, for example on Facebook. The 'wish to return to a past imagined as more ordered might also underlie salsa's global appeal' (Pietrobruno, 2006: 19). This last point is very evident in salsa's gender performances.

Gender Roles and the Global Success of Salsa

Heteronormative[4] constructions of gender are a key aspect in the global success of salsa (see also Schneider, 2013a, 2013b). Gender identity in transnational salsa contexts is a construction that is created in the interaction between Latin and non-Latin people; it is an outcome of global imaginations on the nature of gender in Latin America, and local and national discourses on gender in various other locations. This has effects on dancers and their gender performance, and for me, as a participant observer, gender performance in salsa was the most palpable, in the beginning sometimes unpleasant, aspect of my research experience.

The roles of men and women are very clearly delineated in acting as a dancer. Dancing salsa in contexts that are not clearly defined as 'queer', 'trans', 'gay', 'lesbian' or 'same sex' means that the male dancer decides which steps are taken: he 'leads'. The female dancer follows these decisions, which are mostly indicated by hand and arm moves. In this sense, 'Salsa unabashedly embodies gender hierarchies that characterize the traditional roles of men and women in pre-feminist times' (Pietrobruno, 2006: 19).[5] Such a gender division can be found in most European ballroom dances but is emphasised in a particular way in salsa. The experience of gender hierarchies thus can be disturbing for salsa newcomers. In the beginning, I found it very hard to accept the role that salsa ascribed to me as a woman. The more I learned to dance salsa, however, the more I understood that dancing as a couple would be impossible if both partners decided on the steps and turns to be taken; I therefore also learned that being led in dancing does not necessarily have to be interpreted as a suppression but is a structurally necessary a form of interaction. Being 'led' is different from 'leading'. The 'female' role also has advantages, as it can be enjoyable to 'let go'. Yet, it remains remarkable that it is typically the man who takes decisions and 'leads', while, potentially, people could take turns. Although it sometimes happens that women lead, this is always marked as 'unusual' or 'funny' (Schneider, 2013a).

One reason for salsa's success is most certainly that the gender arrangement makes salsa events a highly structured social activity. People not only appreciate salsa's gender structures because they like to perform masculinity and femininity but also because it facilitates meeting people. There are rules on how to meet and approach each other. Considering that many individuals in contemporary life have to leave their hometowns (or even homelands) for work-related reasons, it is very likely that the opportunity to get to know people in salsa events is an important aspect in understanding the popularity of the dance. This aspect should not be underestimated; however, it is also linked to heteronormative ideology, as meeting people in salsa, above all, means to meet someone of the opposite gender, which is often based on a 'choosing' ritual, where men decide on their female dance partner.[6]

The cultural nostalgia that is produced here is not (as in the case of Latin Americans in diasporic contexts) based on the desire to reconstruct an imagined ethnic identity; it is the reproduction of an imagined gender identity of earlier times. It is, however, not a 'traditional' gender identity associated with German or Australian grandparents, but rather that associated with the culturally 'other' space of salsa, and 'in salsa, it's okay to be a woman' (original quote from a salsa dancer; see also Schneider, 2013b). Stereotypical imagined constructions of Latin American gender roles – for example, Latin American women as 'sexy', pretty, strong and lively – constitute a platform to imagine a past that never existed. The insecurities that come along with the globalisation of culture may be one explanation for the emergence of such nostalgic desires:

> [D]ancers can corporally experience (and find pleasure in) masculine dominance and female submission. The highly fluid nature of global change in the contemporary phase of globalization since the twentieth century has, according to Roland Robertson, nourished the nostalgic tendency for more certain and stable forms of 'world order' (Robertson 1992: 162). This desire for security [...] can lead to a rise in nationalist sentiments to counter what may be perceived as the 'chaos' of transnational fusions and mixtures. This longing for stability in the global arena can also find expression in micropractices of leisure and entertainment such as salsa dance. (Pietrobruno, 2006: 20)

'Regaining' stable ground through fixed and traditional heterosexual gender identity thus is one explanation for the success of salsa in Western urban leisure culture. Yet, the types and degrees of imagination and nostalgia differ in local communities worldwide and also depend on the style of salsa that is appropriated.

Different Styles, Different Identities, Different Ideologies

It is crucial to consider that there are different salsa styles that relate to different discourses and ideologies. Many styles have official names; the most common styles are *ballroom, Cuban, Colombian, New York, Puerto Rican* and *Los Angeles* (*LA*) (Pietrobruno, 2006: 64). Different styles have different histories and convey different ideologies of culture and also of language. Tensions between different styles can be quite strong and '[s]tyle [...] becomes intrinsically bound up with larger social values, beliefs, and practices' (Waxer, 2002b: 6). Dance styles, in this respect, share a lot with language styles, as they are both embedded in holistic concepts of life or *discourses* (see Chapter 2). While for some styles (especially Cuban, Colombian and Puerto Rican), constructions of cultural authenticity and nostalgic imaginations are central, for others, commercial success, cultural innovation and perfection are more important (ballroom, New York and LA) as the latter styles are more strongly influenced by European, competitive show dance culture (Pietrobruno, 2006: ch. 1). It is also important to note that the appropriation of each style can differ across locations. I will not introduce the characteristics of all these styles at this point, as not all are danced in the places where I conducted research. LA-style and Cuban-style salsa figured most prominently in my research contexts and I therefore introduce just these two in more detail.

North American salsa styles such as LA or New York style concentrate on intricate foot choreographies and showy dance moves. In these styles, couples dance on an imaginary line (hence the expression 'on the line'). *Dancing on the line* adds to the comparatively technical impression of these styles. The bodies of couples are usually kept at a distance; only their arms and hands get into contact. LA style is usually danced *on one*, which means that the basic step starts on the first beat of the rhythm. However, some dancers in Sydney also dance LA style *on two*; that is, they dance the first step on the second beat. Dancing *on one* or *on two* does not generally indicate a particular ideology or attitude but is subject to change due to local fashion and the desire to modify the dance from time to time. Overall, apparel, body posture and movements are very similar to dance traditions in European show dance culture and some dance moves involve acrobatics. A central aspect of LA-style salsa are dance competitions, in which more advanced dancers and dance teachers participate and compete (see for example www.australiansalsaopen.com.au). In 2007, during my research fieldwork, the World Salsa Champion was a dancer from Sydney, who regularly appeared in public shows (see www.oliverpineda.com/about-oliver).

In contrast to these showy dance cultures, Cuban-style salsa, at least in the contexts that I observed, foregrounds the experience of dancing as a social and individual experience. Concerning dance moves, Cuban-style salsa focuses on the movements of the body as a whole and Cuban-style dance teachers emphasise that everybody has their own way of moving. Complicated steps and turns can be found but 'holistic body movements', as one interviewee and teacher of this style describes it, are considered more important. Furthermore, the couple engages in circular movements while dancing – Cuban-style salsa is not danced 'on the line'. Cuban style allows for more individual variation than, for example, LA or New York style, which is of course not accidental. The overall discourse on Cuban style as 'authentic' (see Chapter 6), aligned with 'el corazón' and linked to salsa's political background, is related to these 'freer' dance moves. Thus, in salsa, body movements and general attitudes are indexically linked to each other. Yet, it must not be forgotten that local appropriations of these styles – as well as their ideological meanings – can be very different in different places and the above descriptions are only general approaches.

The choice and appropriation of style in the respective locations is related to local histories, where, usually, particular individuals are responsible for the establishment of salsa. At the same time, non-local discourses also influence the success and possibilities of distribution of different styles. Thus, national discourses can be co-responsible for the existence of different salsa styles in different locations. For example, the migration policies of different countries lead to the presence of different cultural groups within one city. Furthermore, the presence of cultural discourses that positively evaluate ethnic authenticity will impact on an interest in 'authentic' Latin salsa (e.g. Cuban or Colombian); discourses with a focus on competition might foster an interest in more competitive styles of salsa (LA, New York). The introduction of different salsa communities in the chapters that follow will illustrate such differences, particularly for the Sydney case, where different communities have developed on the basis of different styles.

Non-professional salsa dancers are often not aware that there are different styles of salsa and may not be aware what the style is called that they themselves dance. Yet, it is noted repeatedly in my interviews that different styles attract different people, although this does not necessarily imply a general consciousness of the ideological distinction between different styles. Some dance schools offer classes in two or more styles, so that their dance pupils will know that there are differences. Dance partners who dance different styles are usually able to dance with each other, as many turns and steps are similar or the same, but if the partner dances a different style, more advanced dancers will notice, even if they are unaware of where the differences arise from. Style differences and the evaluative stance that dancers take towards other styles can play a role in the constitution of different communities (see Chapters 5 and 6 especially).

Having clarified in this chapter the transnational history of salsa, its ties to political and commercial discourses and the creation of transnational cultural spaces that can be observed in non-Latin, Western contexts, the following chapters are each devoted to one community of practice. These communities all have developed on the grounds of different salsa styles, and are partly an outcome of individual preferences, of national discourses and traditions, and of the translocation of culture in a global world.

Notes

(1) Fania, a music label based in New York City, was the most famed producer of salsa music in the 1970s.

(2) Salsa is also popular in non-Western contexts, for example in Japan (Hosokawa, 2002) or Senegal (Stewart, 2000). As my research is limited to Western contexts, I cannot say how audiences in Africa or Asia construct salsa as part of their life-world.

(3) The terms *Latin* and *Latino/a* are used interchangeably in the remainder of the present volume. They refer to people of Latin American descent. Depending on the context, the terms relate not only to pan-American discourses of Latin America but also to the history of the US, where Latin Americans of annexed regions and of migrant origin have a prominent place in political discourse. The usage of the terms in global contexts outside of Latin America is connected to that history. Generally, the term *Latino/a* has to be approached with caution, as it is sometimes considered a pejorative term for lower-class US Americans with Latin American heritage. The term *Hispanic* is also used in US contexts but it emphasises the Spanish rather than the indigenous heritage and is therefore considered less political than *Latino/a* (Pietrobruno, 2006: 108). It will not be used here.

(4) The term *heteronormativity* not only expresses the idea that two (and only two) opposed gender categories exist but also includes normative concepts of sexual desire, above all, the concept of heterosexual love (Hartmann & Klesse, 2007; Motschenbacher, 2011).

(5) There are other forms of salsa dancing, for example group dances, such as *rueda* (where, nevertheless, heterosexual structures are kept); in some cases, groups of female dancers dance with each other.

(6) Although most outsiders assume that there are more women who are eager to learn salsa, my observations cannot confirm this and the number of women and men seems to be roughly equal.

4 'Das macht mich immer fröhlich wenn ich Spanisch sprechen kann'. Multilingual Longing and Class Exclusion in Frankfurt's Salsa Community

Frankfurt salsa is a vivid example of the interplay of global imaginations and national discourses in local appropriations of transnational culture. The quote in Box 4.1 reveals language ideologies as I encountered them frequently in Frankfurt salsa. A native speaker of German practically destabilises national ideologies of language by constructing emotional ties to an 'other' language. At the same time, the utterance tacitly reflects

Box 4.1 Language ideology in Frankfurt salsa

Das macht mich immer fröhlich
wenn ich Spanisch sprechen kann, total (.)
das find ich total klässe (1.5)
ich weiss auch nich,
ja, es is schwer zu sagen, was es eigentlich is (2)
doch so'n bisschen (1)
ja wirklich, dieses aus der eigenen Rolle (1)
der unterkühlten Mitteleuropäerin bisschen aus (.) zu (.) dingsen.

It always makes me happy
when I can speak Spanish, absolutely,
I find it absolutely thrilling (1.5)
I don't know,
yes, it is difficult to say, what it actually is (2)
but a little bit (1)
yes, really, this out-of-the-own role (1)
of the frosty middle European a little bit, to break out of it.

See p. ix for transcription conventions.

German discourses of belonging, which are still characterised by 'Herderian' views – the idea that a *language* and a *Volk* and its 'worldview' are intrinsically, almost naturally, linked. A more thorough analysis of such discourses requires ethnographic insights into local practice.

As I conducted research in Germany before I observed the Australian communities, I begin the presentation of the empirical data in this volume with the Frankfurt salsa community. I first present some general background information on national discourses on language and ethnicity in Germany, and secondly I introduce ethnographic observations on salsa in Frankfurt, before turning to observations more specifically concerned with language. Afterwards, I give an analysis of selected interview data on discursive constructions of language as found in the community. The analysis is divided into two sections, one devoted to language ideologies of German salsa dancers related to Spanish, the other to language discourse pertaining to less desired 'others'. The final section of the chapter links empirical data to the research questions set out in Chapter 1.

German Public Discourses on Multilingualism and Multiculturalism

In comparison with traditional immigration countries like Australia or the US, German public and governmental discourses concerning migration, integration and language are characterised by comparatively strong monocultural and also monolingual tendencies. Generally, German laws on citizenship and their consequences for ideologies of culture, language and belonging were among the most conservative in the European context until citizenship laws changed in 2000 (on these new laws, see Reißlandt, 2006: 153–156). The causes for that are to be found in the historical development of Germany. The ethnic *Volk* nation was an ideological basis for the formation of the state, which came into being as late as 1870. Moreover, Germany played only a very marginal role as a coloniser and thus did not create citizens who reside in colonies. As a result, citizenship policy was based on the *jus sanguinis* until 2000 (Koopmans, 2001). In the idea of the German *Volk* as a 'biologically' related group of people, the role of language has always been salient. Language serves as symbol and affirmation of the proclaimed organic entity (Barbour & Carmichael, 2000; Blommaert & Verschueren, 1998: 195). Thus, even today, language policies and discourses on language often tacitly (but also openly) reproduce monocultural and assimilationist ideologies in contemporary German discourses and essentialist concepts of 'German-hood' prevail in many contexts (see also Stevenson & Mar-Molinero, 2006b).

Although counter-discourses are vital, it is easy to find examples from contemporary German public discourse that illustrate the normalisation of ethnic essentialism and institutional racism. Some recent high-impact academic publications that were subject to lively debates (and were generally not considered to be right wing) demonstrate the acceptance of discourses of nationalist character (see especially Buschkowsky, 2012; Sarrazin, 2010). Such contributions continue to conceive of ethnic minorities as 'non-German' and to draw an image of 'over-Islamisation' due to 'multicultural' and lax policies that supposedly 'threaten' German culture.[1] This reveals racially categorised discourses in which people operate and which are often part of common-sense knowledge and therefore difficult to overcome. These are interwoven with ideologies of language and with language policies.

A rather obvious example for monolingual ideology is the *German-only* policy of many schools and kindergartens, where it is forbidden to use any language other than German (*Spiegel Online*, 2006). Another example from the educational realm is that in some federal states, children whose language competence in German is rated as poor have to attend a one-year German course and are not allowed to attend regular schooling (Reißlandt, 2006: 156) – a policy that is regarded as highly discriminatory in many other countries; in the UK, for example, such practices have been proscribed for over 30 years (see e.g. Bullock, 1975). It is often argued that the maintenance of ethnic minority languages is a sign of a 'lack of integration' into the German majority society. Bilingual classes with languages spoken by minorities – Turkish, Italian, Arabic or languages from former Yugoslavia – are common only in some urban areas (it is difficult to give a concise overview due to the federal education system, for the respective *Länder*, see Gogolin *et al.*, 2001). Numerous examples, particularly from newspaper articles, show that public discourse constructs it as self-evident that bilingualism, if not acquired in a formal context, leads to school difficulties (see Stevenson & Schanze, 2009) and that schools with a high number of bilingual pupils are of poor quality (for more, see e.g. Gogolin, 2001).

The monolingual habitus (Gogolin, 1994) of German state institutions, however, does not relate to schooling for German elites. Language learning is very high on the agenda of German school curricula, and for German children bilingual classes with prestige languages like French and English have become popular within recent years (see e.g. Wolff, 2007). Multilingual competence that has been acquired in formal contexts has a high prestige. 'Instrumental bilingualism' (Hoffmann, 1991) with popular standard languages, as found in German high schools, is seen an asset on global markets and is not considered to touch on constructions of ethnic identity. German national discourses on language also have to be considered in the context of the geopolitical situation of Germany within Europe. In comparison with Australia, say, from Germany, travel to other European countries is inexpensive and therefore common. Learning the languages of European neighbours is often considered to be important. Additionally, language learning plays a key role in the language policies of the European Union (EU), which have the goal of establishing trilingualism in all European citizens (see e.g. Commission of the European Communities, 2005). Thus, German discourses on language are embedded in a European discourse on multilingualism in a culturally diverse political arrangement.

Germany has officially abandoned ethnic nationalism and the *jus sanguinis* but monocultural ideologies are often tacitly maintained in the guise of monolingual, assimilationist ideology. On the face of it, the goal of this ideology might seem to be a monolingual society. However, looking more closely at different policies for different cohorts of the population and at multilingual realities in German cities, the picture becomes much more multifaceted. As data from salsa communities suggest, in an era of cultural globalisation and transnational cultural development, discourses on language, culture and 'integration' do not construct simple 'either/or' distinctions but relate to complex linguistic and cultural hierarchies, while they can nevertheless continue to reconstruct essentialist positions. We will start accessing these complex hierarchies by considering some general insights into the community.

Ethnographic Observations on Frankfurt Salsa

Germany-wide, salsa is highly popular; salsa communities are found in all the bigger cities. Frankfurt has a relatively long salsa tradition and several informants told me that salsa arrived in Frankfurt during the 1980s, as a side-effect of the occupation of Germany after the Second World War. Until the 1990s, a large number of US American soldiers resided in the Rhein–Main area, where the biggest military airport outside the US used to be located after US forces invaded Germany in 1945. According to my interviewees, soldiers of Puerto Rican background were the first to dance salsa in Frankfurt, in a venue called Brotfabrik.

Today, there are many salsa classes in Frankfurt. There are two schools devoted to salsa only and about ten schools that offer salsa classes in addition to others. Next to dance schools, there are, in Sydney as in Frankfurt, venues that offer salsa 'nights', salsa parties. Salsa nights typically begin with an introductory class that is offered before the actual party starts. These courses are usually beginners' courses that allow newcomers to participate in the party later on. In Frankfurt and Sydney alike, there are, furthermore,

Figure 4.1 Example of a website promoting a Frankfurt salsa venue and party (www.latinpalace-chango.de/index.php?id=43, from 16 September 2013)

Latin bars that play salsa but also other Latin music. Salsa parties or Latin venues (Figure 4.1) aim at the creation of a 'Latin' atmosphere, for example by selling drinks associated with Latin culture, such as Corona beer and cocktails like mojito, Cuba libre, or also caipirinha (which is Brazilian but nevertheless perceived as 'Latin').

Salsa venues are often decorated with straw, reminiscent of a beach hut. 'Latinness' is sometimes produced through visual images that relate to Cuba's communist regime – typically, walls are decorated with Cuban flags (although flags from other Latin American countries also often appear), red stars and pictures of the Cuban (Argentine-born) communist national hero Che Guevara. The presence of Cuban symbols is not an accident, as many Frankfurt salsa dancers have an inclination to left-wing discourses and perceive Cuba and its regime relatively positively. They often adhere to the dichotomy of 'US capitalism' (considered to be negative) versus 'Latin

American *corazón'* (considered to be positive), similar to the construction found in salsa's history (see Chapter 3). At the same time, the political significance of such communist symbols must not be over-interpreted, as many salsa dancers may understand them as more or less neutral symbols of 'Latin' culture, used on a capitalist market to construct a 'Latin' branding.

On the local level, Frankfurt's salsa community is structured differently from salsa communities in Sydney (see Chapters 5 and 6). Frankfurt is smaller than Sydney and, despite internal divisions, and despite dancers' and places' differences in ideological orientation, I consider salsa in Frankfurt to constitute only one community of practice. As the city is rather small (600,000 inhabitants), there is not a large number of salsa clubs. In the city, ethnic communities are not clearly segregated according to place. Salsa dancers from different ethnic backgrounds and those who dance different styles come together in the same places. Some differences between Frankfurt and Sydney are an outcome of activities of individuals who have their particular contacts, personal histories or preferences. For example, LA style is not danced in Frankfurt but, instead, New York style has here the function of the 'performative', 'stiff' style, which, according to my informants, is the result of individual dance teachers' and dance school owners' preferences. Cuban-style salsa is, overall, more popular in Frankfurt than in Sydney (see Chapter 3 for a more detailed description of the different styles).

Cuban style's popularity in Frankfurt is largely an effect of the personal decisions of dance school owners but, at the same time, may also be a result of a stronger German affinity to discourses of ethnic authenticity. This interpretation relies on the experiences I had in Sydney, where salsa dancers do not necessarily interpret salsa as a 'Latin' and 'cultural' thing (see Chapters 5 and 6). When I started fieldwork in Germany, I did not regard the desire of German salsa dancers to participate in something culturally 'authentic' as being based in German discourses. I assumed this to be an effect of access to Latin culture and I also thought Cuban salsa to be the 'normal' style. Having had access to only German salsa culture at this point, I was not aware of my own conceptualisation of salsa as 'Latin'. In general, it is of course difficult to give a definite answer to the question why Cuban salsa is popular in Frankfurt, but the example shows that cross-national comparison can be enlightening in this respect.

My first visits to salsa locations were characterised by the experiences related to gender performance that I introduced in Chapter 3. Next to my struggles to handle the position allocated to me as a woman in salsa parties, the frequent interaction between people who did not know each other beforehand and the inclusiveness of salsa events struck me as remarkable (Box 4.2). People of different age groups and different ethnic and cultural

Box 4.2 Field note, 16 August 2006, Brotfabrik

When entering the room, I am again surprised that the whole room is just prepared for dancing, there is no room for activities other than dancing, except for standing next to the dance-floor and watching. The people who have come here are of all ages, the youngest maybe 25 and the oldest around 50 or maybe even 60. [...] The usually very inclusive setting is nice but I still feel that there is something artificial, stylised and also conservative, conventional in this way of spending leisure time.

backgrounds participate in most of the parties. It is, in any case, a lot easier than in many other social contexts to approach and get to know people at salsa parties (see also Chapter 3).

The setting is inclusive not only in terms of in age but also in terms of ethnicity. It is enlightening to consider the ethnic background of informants. Although I do not intend to reproduce social boundaries as ethnic boundaries, ethnic boundaries are highly vital in German discourses and therefore cannot be ignored. Members of Frankfurt's salsa community are Latin Americans, 'mainstream' Germans and of diverse African, Turkish, Arabic, Greek and other southern European descent.

While taking pleasure in the dance is one thing that all salsa dancers share, irrespective of age, gender and ethnicity, there are different desires that bring people to salsa. Germans feel attracted by salsa as they regard it as an exotic 'other' activity that brings along a lot of positive associations and emotions (see below in this chapter). Germans in Frankfurt salsa typically have a rather high educational background and can be considered 'middle class'. Similar to what has been described in Chapter 3, Latin Americans very often become salsa aficionados or 'Latinos' only after they have arrived in Germany (see also Papadopoulos, 2003). Generally, being 'Latin' is of positive value in Germany and, in contrast to other ethnic backgrounds, particularly Turkish or Arab, Latin descent is not necessarily marked in a negative way. One reason for that may be political discourses of the 1970s, where a German left-wing culture emerged that supported political refugees from Latin American dictatorial regimes. German discourse typically does not construct Latin Americans as coming to Germany to exploit the social welfare system and, in the 1970s, Latin American refugees often had a middle-class background and/or were romanticised as left-wing revolutionaries (see e.g. www.ila-bonn.de/verschiedenes/ila.htm; on the history of immigration from Latin America to Germany, see Kohut, 1996).

The positive connotations German discourses convey with regard to Latin culture make salsa parties an attractive location for non-Latin 'foreigners'. On the basis of participant observation, it is impossible to give even a low-key quantification of the ethnic distribution in salsa events, as the ethnic background of the dancers cannot be ascertained from their looks. I refrained from asking dancers about their 'real' background and the phenotype of the dancers is not indicative of their ethnicity. In salsa, the way somebody looks does not necessarily mark whether a person stems from, for example, Sudan or Cuba, which allows dancers to perform a Latin identity irrespective of citizenship or heritage, especially for those who are often rejected by mainstream German nightclubs. It is especially males who seem to be engaged in a form of ethnic mimicry (Bhabha, 1994) to perform an ethnic identity that is locally of higher cultural value than their own ethnic background.

During my research, I saw many and danced with some male individuals of African and Arab descent who I had first thought to be Latinos. Some of these 'others' have acquired Spanish and thus also perform a linguistic identity that is of higher cultural capital than their 'original' ethnicity in the German context. The identification with Spanish in one case went as far as renaming – during the time of my research, there was an ethnic Afghan in Frankfurt who introduced himself with a Spanish name (see also Papadopoulos, 2003).

It is symptomatic of this value of ethnic Latin authenticity that there was one venue in Frankfurt (*Living*, in the summer of 2007) that gave free entrance to people with Latin American passports on salsa nights. Having real 'Latinos' and 'Latinas' at a salsa party increases the 'authentic' value of the event and the owners of most clubs seem to want to avoid having too many non-Latin 'others'. Selling the image of the 'real Latin lover' was part of the marketing strategy of the Living club, but it was also a strategy of racial segregation in differentiating between Latin people and people of other (undesired) ethnic descent.

This hints at the construction of a transnational hierarchy, constructed in a local environment, in which some cultures carry positive connotations and some are regarded more negatively (as 'poor', 'dangerous', 'fanatic', etc.). The desire of 'other' ethnicities to cross to Latin ethnicity and to the Spanish language is simultaneously indicative of such a transnational hierarchy and of German structures of exclusion. This interpretation links to the language ideologies in the community, to which I introduce some language-related ethnographic data in the following section.

Language in Frankfurt Salsa

Frankfurt's salsa community is a German-speaking context with a relatively high usage of the Spanish language. The medium of education in Frankfurt salsa contexts is German; German was spoken in all four 8-week dance courses I attended. Nevertheless, the Spanish language can always be heard in salsa venues. Above all, this is a result of the music played. The music and the songs that are listened to are predominantly in Spanish[2] and mostly stem from the transnational Latin space that has been introduced above (Chapter 3). Dance moves in the salsa classes I attended were introduced, with a few exceptions, with Spanish names. Additionally, as people from the Latin American continent are usually present in Frankfurt salsa, Spanish is also heard frequently in conversations. Many dance teachers stem from Latin America, and most DJs in parties are Latin, as are some dancers.

Some other Spanish language items and Latin discourse phenomena can be detected. Latin American greeting formulas are common, also among people of non-Latin descent. Many times, my informants greeted me by saying *hola* (hello) and gave me two kisses on the cheek, which is not common in German contexts, at least not with people one has never met before. It happened to me several times that Latin American men who approached me and asked me for a dance started to speak to me in Spanish, although they did not know whether I spoke the language or not. Many parties are advertised as *fiestas* (Spanish for 'party'), and party flyers and posters often include phrases like *una noche de salsa* ('a night of salsa') or *salsa caliente* ('hot salsa') (even a casual web search will highlight a large number of pages that feature such phrases). I also saw several posters and flyers in salsa schools that promoted salsa trips to Cuba, on which Spanish is learned in the morning and salsa in the afternoon.

Most salsa dancers in Frankfurt have a very positive attitude towards Spanish. German salsa aficionados are interested not only in meeting to dance but typically also in the acquisition of Spanish. In contrast to the Sydney example (Chapters 5 and 6), no Frankfurt interviewee reported the Spanish language to be irrelevant, while all agreed that it is a desirable component of the salsa experience. The acquisition of Spanish here cannot be understood as having an instrumental function in the sense that it would, for example, be helpful in getting a job. For most, it rather seems a crucial tool in the production and performance of a particular type of identity.

On grounds of these observations and also of the interview contents (see below), I consider the function of Spanish in this context to be a form a linguistic cosmopolitanism. As has been introduced in Chapter 2, Ulf Hannerz's anthropological concept conceives of cosmopolitanism as 'an orientation, a willingness to engage with the Other [...], a search for contrasts rather than uniformity' (Hannerz, 1996a: 103). A search for cultural contrasts is obvious in the Frankfurt salsa community. A second point where Frankfurt salsa practices relate to Hannerz's concept is that, in his understanding, cosmopolitan engagement with other cultures is based on the idea of intention, rather than need (Hannerz, 1996a: 105ff.). Salsa dancers in Frankfurt typically do not have any existential need to learn Spanish; their engagement with the language is clearly intentional. The function of such an intention is the production of a class-based position that demonstrates cultural mobility and access to a meta-level of culture. It allows one to be differentiated from 'locals', who are regarded as static and as having access to only one culture. Establishing a transnational middle-class position on grounds of cultural and linguistic mobility is certainly a crucial aspect in understanding Frankfurt salsa dancers' desires to learn Spanish.

This is also an effect of discourses on language learning in Germany, where speaking English is not enough to show cosmopolitan intentions. As it is compulsory in Germany to learn at least one language at school, which is English in most cases, it is considered 'normal' to speak English *and* German. German–English bilingualism is not a marker of distinction. In a German setting, a third language, especially a positively connoted language like Spanish, therefore serves as symbol for higher education and cultural capital, and produces a 'cosmopolitan' identity. Accordingly, there are quite a number of salsa dancers who speak Spanish fluently (according to my data, which is, however, not representative, about a third of the Frankfurt salsa population speaks Spanish fluently, either as a native speaker or as a second language speaker). Given that learning the Spanish language is considered a form of linguistic cosmopolitanism, it does not come as a surprise that dancers who do not speak Spanish usually excuse this lack of ability by explaining that they plan to learn the language in the future, or at least maintain that they would like to do it.

In theory, the outcome of multilingual practices and identifications in Frankfurt salsa could be hybrid or 'translingual' identities (see Chapter 2). Yet, it must not be forgotten that the construction of cosmopolitanism as observed here relies on the presence of cultural 'others', who are usually conceived of as traditional and static. Interview statements from Frankfurt salsa dancers suggest that informants, despite their attempt to participate in an 'other' cultural discourse, reconstruct ethnic boundaries as essential. To get a closer understanding of such intricacies of transnational language discourse between hybridity and essentialism, in the following section I analyse discursive data from interviews with salsa dancers in more detail.

Aspirating 'Latinness', Reproducing Ethnic Boundaries

The analysis of interview data shows that Spanish-speaking German salsa dancers create transnational ties through their cosmopolitan intentions. At the same time, native German salsa dancers often explain their desire to speak Spanish with reference to discourses of ethnicity and thus tacitly reproduce national language ideology (see Chapter 2). Simultaneous processes of crossing (Rampton, 1995a; see also Chapter 2) and of reconstructing ethnic and linguistic boundaries makes discourses on language in Frankfurt's salsa community a highly enlightening example for developing a critical perspective on transnational and translingual theory.

As has been mentioned, German interviewees do not relate their acquisition of Spanish to, for example, the desire to enhance their job chances due to language skills. Furthermore, they do not describe competence in Spanish as vital in belonging to a transnational salsa world. Language is here not primarily regarded as an instrument of communication. While in public German discourse, learning of other languages by Germans is not usually discussed in terms of identity (see above) but mainly in terms of instrumentality and prestige, this is different in salsa contexts. Here, the language Spanish is strongly associated with categories of personal and ethnic identity.

The desire to 'become someone else', also in ethnic terms, is a central element in several interview passages. This indexes a construction of the self as an (ethnic) 'other', which is linked to stereotypical (German) discourses on Latin American identity. Native German respondents thus relate the Spanish language to personal emotions, but also to a questioning of their German identity, as in this first quote from an interview with a female German salsa dancer:

> Ich hab schon das Gefühl (.)
> das macht mich immer fröhlich
> wenn ich Spanisch sprechen kann, total (.)
> das find ich total klásse (1.5)
> ich weiss auch nich,
> ja, es is schwer zu sagen, was es eigentlich is (2)
> doch so'n bisschen (1)
> ja wirklich, dieses aus der eigenen Rolle (1)
> der unterkühlten Mitteleuropäerin bisschen aus (.) zu (.) dingsen. (A 13)[3]

I do have the feeling (.)
it always makes me happy
when I can speak Spanish, absolutely,
I find it absolutely thrilling (1.5)
I don't know,
yes, it is difficult to say, what it actually is (2)
but a little bit (1)
yes, really, this out-of-the-own-role (1)
of the frosty middle European a little bit (.) to break out (.) of it.

The interviewee maintains that speaking Spanish makes her feel very joyful and happy and she places a strong emphasis on this by pronouncing the words 'total' (absolutely) and 'klasse' (thrilling) louder and with stress. She then ponders on the reasons for that and her utterance includes quite a few hesitating pauses; it seems difficult to explain her feelings. The reason that she eventually gives is that, in speaking Spanish, she feels she breaks out of a role that is given to her by other social discourses: the role of the 'frosty middle European'.

First of all, it is interesting that the informant here does not consider her identity to be native German but she identifies as 'Mitteleuropäerin'. It is unclear where the concept of the 'frosty middle European' stems from. German identity is stereotypically overly serious and socially 'cold', while the concept of 'middle European identity' is not at all common in everyday discourse. It may be speculated that the interviewee's various travels to Cuba have brought about an awareness of categorisations of 'European-ness' in Latin American discourses. As US Americans, due to historical–political reasons, have a rather negative image in Latin America (see Chapter 3; and McPherson, 2006), the category 'European' here serves as an opportunity for tourists from Europe to differentiate from *gringos*, US citizens.

An awareness of the gaze of the 'other', indicating access to a cultural meta-discourse, here demonstrates a cosmopolitanism position (Hannerz, 1996a). On the other hand, the widespread stereotype of Germans as orderly, strict and stiff (see e.g. many internet sources) may also increase the desire of this German to 'break out' of her culture of origin. She constructs a binary dichotomy of 'middle European' as frosty and of Hispanic cultures as its opposite. Further, the interviewee feels the Spanish language not only indexes happiness but also evokes feelings of happiness in herself. Speaking Spanish here creates a possibility for the speaker to construct an identity that is different from the one that was inherited through geographical location and family ties. Yet, the existence of ethnic and linguistic boundaries is not questioned.

The impression that the Spanish language is closely tied to positive emotions is also found in other interview passages. In this second example, another German female salsa dancer mentions the ease with which emotions can be expressed in Spanish, and considers this to be a vital element for her positive attitudes towards the language:

> Also wenn ich Spanisch spreche (1)
> das macht mich immer unheimlich glücklich
> das macht mich unheimlich frei (.).
> Ja, viele Sachen sind viel einfacher.
> Vor allem über Gefühle zu reden (.).
> Ja, und ich komm auch immer in so 'ne (1.5)
> relativ schnell in so 'ne aufgedrehte glückliche Stimmung. (I 4)
>
> Well, when I speak Spanish (1)
> it always makes me immensely happy
> it makes me immensely free (.).
> Yes, many things are a lot easier.
> Especially to speak about emotions (.).
> Yes, and I always get into (1.5)
> relatively quickly, into an energetic, happy mood.

Speaking Spanish is here described as evoking positive feelings of happiness and, also, of freedom (interestingly, this function of Spanish was never mentioned in the Sydney data set). The interviewee maintains that communication about feelings is easier in Spanish, which is related to the idea that speaking Spanish makes the informant feel 'free'. It is difficult to clarify why the informant thinks that feelings can be expressed more easily in Spanish than in German. One reason may be that in the lyrics of salsa songs from the era of *salsa romántica* (see Chapter 3), there is indeed a tendency to constantly report on emotions of love or of unanswered love. Whether a tendency to speak more openly about feelings is particular to such salsa songs, or is also found in everyday discourses in Latin America, where the informant had spent a lot of time, as her husband stemmed from Colombia, remains speculative. Possibly, a German-derived stereotypical image of the Latin lover influences the idea.

In the two quotes above, using Spanish serves as a tool to perform an 'other' identity. Besides its interpretation as a form of cosmopolitanism, it is reminiscent of Rampton's observations on language crossing in British educational contexts (see Chapter 2; and Rampton, 1995a), where adopting another language can create liminal moments. Rampton describes liminality as 'moments and activities, when the ordered flow of habitual social life [is] loosened and when normal social relations [can]not be taken for granted' (Rampton, 1995a: 281). Similar things seem to happen here, particularly in the interviewees' statements regarding a change of mood due to linguistic choice, and in considering language as a way to 'break out' in constructing an identity that is different from the 'normal' one. Spanish takes the function of a type of Shangri-La;[4] it has utopian elements in that it serves for German salsa dancers as a tool to perform an 'other' identity.

This 'other' identity is made possible through accessing discourses that do not traditionally belong to the local or national environment, including the 'other's' gaze on oneself, which involves stereotypes of Germans as strict, orderly and rude. Access to discourses from other cultures and places here brings about a desire to be 'different' in an ethnic sense. However, the national scale is co-responsible for such a position, as the indexical ties of the Spanish language with the quality of being 'emotional', 'free' and 'happy' are also an outcome of German imaginations of Latin American culture. Additionally, stereotypes of Germans may be related to discourses that are actually present in Germany.

Overall, German salsa dancers' usage of Spanish seems to fulfil desires to participate in practices and emotions of an 'other' culture, which creates liminal moments of distance with regard to German culture. These are vital in demonstrating cultural mobility and in creating a cosmopolitan position. Although such practices overcome national and cultural boundaries in the appropriation of discourses from other places, they are at the same time related to nostalgic aspirations that reconstruct cultural boundaries as 'real'. Despite their enthusiasm for Latin culture and their desire to speak Spanish, interviewees generally assume that it is not possible to truly 'cross' ethnic boundaries, as the following female salsa dancer's quote on her desire to speak 'accent-free' Spanish confirms:

> Ich würd's echt gerne perfektionieren,
> ja und es ist wahrscheinlich auch der Wunsch von jedem (1)
> ähm, der irgendwie so Spanisch lernt, (.)
> dass man's halt irgendwann möglichst akzentfrei spricht
> und von den, von den Latinos (2)
> na ja gut, als ihresgleichen aufgenommen wird man wahrscheinlich nicht. (lacht) (A 23)
>
> I would love to perfect it,
> yes, and it is probably also the desire of everybody (1)
> uhm, who learns Spanish (.)

> that one day you speak without an accent
> and to be, by the Latinos (2)
> well, to be accepted, as one among them, this will probably not happen. (laughs)

The informant firstly assumes that 'everybody' who learns Spanish has the desire to speak the language with a native accent (on the ideology of language without accent, see Lippi-Green, 1997), which relates to the desire to 'become someone else' and to 'break out' of given cultural identities. Speaking a second language without a non-native accent means that interlocutors will assume that one 'truly' belongs to the community of native speakers of that language. This community is, nevertheless, seen as (probably) out of reach for non-native speakers.

Interestingly, the desire to speak a non-native language 'accent-free' was never mentioned in the Australian context. German discourses on ethnic authenticity, which still rely on traditional ideas of ethnicity and belonging, may be co-responsible for the popularity of essentialist longing in a German context. The construction of individuals as 'naturally' belonging to a culture is partly based on language ideologies in which language serves for authentic affiliation with that culture (see also Chapter 2). The same construction is found in the above quote. German ideologies of essentialism not only made naturalisation of immigrants a difficult endeavour until the year 2000 (see above), but are also connected to the demand that migrants have a good command of German if they want to gain German citizenship today (see e.g. Möllering, 2010; Stevenson & Schanze, 2009). These ideologies are related to a German interviewee having the ambition to 'perfect' her Spanish, which is synonymous with 'authentic' native language competence.

Learning a language perfectly, 'without an accent', is a common desire of Germans learning other languages, including English. Negative images of German identity, based on Germany's history, can be assumed to be a second vital factor in Germans' desire to conceal their identity in non-German contexts. Although I have often met non-Germans who were surprised by this, as a German I can closely relate to feelings of unease about being German. While others typically assume that the Third Reich has nothing to do with younger generations, it is not so far away if your grandfather was a member of the SS or if Auschwitz survivors leave the room when you speak because they cannot stand to hear German.[5]

Essentialist language ideologies, perfectionism and German history all add to a German desire to learn languages 'without an accent'. In the quote above, the interviewee constructs this desire as common sense. Afterwards, she starts the sentence 'and to be, by the Latinos…' and then interrupts herself. She obviously intended to say that the underlying motivation of accent-free Spanish would be to be regarded as a Latina, but, after a pause, she corrects herself and says that the ethnic 'other' would not accept Germans as part of their community, even if those Germans were able to speak Spanish 'without an accent'. These native Germans strive to be as 'Latin' as possible, although they assume that a complete 'passing' as ethnically 'other' is impossible. In terms of attitudes towards ethnic essentialism and the possibility and impossibility of becoming part of another culture, there are striking differences with the Australian data.

Taking into account German historical discourses on language and nationalism, it is not really surprising that German respondents describe shifts in ethnic identity as basically impossible. Simultaneously, the desire to speak the 'other' language as perfectly as possible relates to a valorisation of ethnic authenticity (on constructions of authenticity and their relevance for language discourse, see e.g. Lacoste & Mair, 2012; Schneider, 2014). The value of authenticity results in a high status of Latin people within the local salsa community. In Frankfurt salsa, people from the Latin American continent are reported to feel superior on the basis of their ethnicity:

> Zu den Latinos passt man sowieso nicht,
> die ja sowieso irgendwie ihre mehr oder minder (1.5)
> Enklave da noch bilden (.)
> und da auch die Leute eigentlich gar nicht so wirklich reinlassen,
> beziehungsweise, wir sind hier die Latinos
> und ihr seit hier halt schon so die Deutschen,
> die halt hier so tanzen
> und wenn ihr das gut macht, dann ist das schon cool,
> aber najà. (A 4)
>
> One does not match with the Latinos anyways,
> who anyways somehow more or less (1.5)
> build their own enclave (.)
> and who do not really allow other people to enter,
> or, we are here, the Latinos
> and you over there, you are just the Germans,
> who just dance around here and when you are good in it, then it is pretty cool,
> but, well.

'Authentic' ethnicity functions as symbolic capital in this context. Dancing well increases one's status as a dancer, but 'real' Latin American ethnicity functions as a boundary marker. In this quote, the salsa community in Frankfurt is described as a divided community, but, in contrast to the Sydney case (see Chapters 5 and 6), it is not the style of dance that divides the dancers but ethnic descent. It is interesting to note that the 'foreigners', the 'Latinos', are not described as attempting to belong to German society or an ethnically mixed community of practice. Rather, they are seen as consciously separating from the rest, as building an 'enclave' within the community.

In other interviews, Cubans in particular are described as having the tendency to produce ethnic pride and cultural separatism within the Latin community. Whether this is an effect of Cuban essentialist discourses or of German essentialist discourses, constructing 'becoming German' as almost unachievable, is not possible to conclude from the data. In any case, it is notable that ethnic Latin Americans are described as part of the salsa community but nevertheless essentially different due to their ethnic background. This shows that boundaries between cultures, ethnic groups and languages are traversed but not destabilised.

While the construction of other cultures as 'different', 'static' and therefore 'not developed' is typical with reference to, for example, indigenous cultures, and as also occurs in relation to Latin Americans in Sydney salsa, Latin Americans' ethnic background in the Frankfurt case is given a high symbolic status. Although German interviewees ascribe romanticised notions of emotionality and happiness to Latin culture and the Spanish language, Latin American culture is not constructed as 'underdeveloped'. Through being understood as 'authentic', Latin Americans in this German salsa setting gain social status, from which they also profit economically as dance teachers, musicians or DJs. However, not all Latin Americans are perceived so positively. Some data reveal class prejudice, resulting in a language ideology that reflects German public discourses on the 'lack of integration' of foreigners.

Intersections of National Language Ideology and Class Exclusion

A sub-group of Latin Americans in the salsa community of Frankfurt is, despite their Latin origin, sometimes considered negatively. Interestingly, while a lack of German was no issue with reference to Cubans or other Latin Americans, Colombian refugees' allegedly poor German is sometimes considered a problem. Such contradictions show that language ideologies on immigrants and their linguistic integration are understandable only in a complex hierarchy of ethnic–class intersections. This hierarchy has various causes. The Cubans I met in Frankfurt had a high educational attainment, were trained musicians, classical dancers or had studied at university and were not perceived negatively, irrespective of their language competence. It is thus not only their 'authenticity' but, presumably, also their education that gives them a high status in the community of practice. Next to this local condition, German essentialist discourses, transnational discourses on the relative economic, social and political standing of other nations and the interaction between such discourses have to be considered as co-constructive of local ethnic–class intersections.

A negative rating of Colombians occurred only once in my interviews; yet, informal conversations and other ethnographic texts reveal that Colombians with refugee background who spend their free time in salsa venues have a rather negative image in the community of practice. There is a prejudiced assumption that Colombian women generally work in red-light districts or have married German men in order to gain a residence permit (see also Papadopoulos, 2003: 93). Although my informants also reported that there are other Latin Americans, particularly men, whose German is very poor, it is only with regard to Colombians that a lack of language skills is problematised.

The language competence of economically marginal speakers of either German or Spanish might not adhere to standardised norms. However, it may be assumed that the economically marginal position of refugees is another cause for the representation of Colombians as linguistically deficient. In the context of another ethnographic research project on salsa in Frankfurt, a native German speaker describes Colombians as not speaking German:

> Frankfurt hat ja natürlich auch eine spezielle Szene,
> die auch leider sehr viel mit Kolumbianern zu tun hat.
> Und diese Szene speziell,
> oder diese Kolumbianer,
> die reden,
> also die können auch kein deutsch sprechen,
> ja, leben eigentlich nur unter sich selber.
>
> Frankfurt has, of course, a special scene,
> which unfortunately has to do much with Colombians.
> And this scene especially,
> or these Colombians,
> they speak,
> well, they can't speak German,
> actually only live among themselves.
> (M, see Papadopoulos, 2003: 93)

The image that is produced here resembles closely the one that is produced in public German discourses that have been introduced above, where diversity is usually seen as obstructing a cohesive society. Certain cohorts of 'foreigners', *Ausländer*, are represented as people who cannot speak German and do not mix with others. Maintenance of cultures and languages other than German is often understood as threatening to create *Parallelgesellschaften*, 'parallel societies' (see e.g. Halm & Sauer, 2006). However, it is generally considered 'better' to speak Spanish and German than, for example, Turkish and German. Spanish-speaking minorities are not subject to public discourse, whereas a language ideological discourse on the lack of German is frequent in relation to the Turkish minority in Germany.

It is striking to note that during the course of all Frankfurt interviews, when it comes to the question of multilingualism in Germany, all informants start to talk about the Turkish minority. The claim that 'the Turks' – *die Türken* – are those who are unwilling to learn German and who are therefore problematic is frequent, as in the following quote from a native German salsa dancer:

> Ja natürlich gibt es da schon auch Probleme hier in Deutschland,
> mit den Leuten, die sich nicht integrieren wollen,
> wie ja zum Beispiel die Türken,
> die kein Deutsch lernen.
> Das ist natürlich total respektlos. (I 27)
>
> Yes, sure, there are problems, here in Germany,
> with those who do not want to integrate,
> like, for example, the Turks(,)
> who don't learn German.
> This is of course very disrespectful.

The interviewee here produces a 'common-sense' discourse in saying that, 'natürlich', 'naturally' or 'sure', there are problems with those who do not want to 'integrate'. Although the notion of integration is rarely defined, the accusation that 'foreigners' are unwilling to 'integrate' is a widespread belief in German public discourse and the effects of this construct on individual attitudes have been documented in other ethnographic studies (e.g. Gruner, 2010). In German public discourses, Germans of Turkish descent often function as a symbol for presumed social problems with 'integration'. They are the biggest minority in Germany, numbering approximately two million. It is therefore not unexpected that the interviewee here refers to 'die Türken' in relating to language-related problems in Germany.

The modal particle 'ja' in 'wie ja zum Beispiel die Türken' shows that the speaker supposes that the consideration of Turks being a problem is shared by the hearer. She constructs common ground and assumes this attitude to be universally valid. From the syntactic construction of the sentence 'die Türken, die kein Deutsch lernen' ('the Turks[,] who don't learn German') it is unclear whether she here produces a restrictive or a non-restrictive relative clause.[6] It is thus unclear whether she intends to say that Turks generally do not learn German, or whether she here refers only to those Turks who do not learn the language. In any case, she constructs a 'matter of fact' image of the idea that there are problems with Turks who do not learn German and then concludes that this behaviour is 'of course' disrespectful.

The fact that all respondents from the Frankfurt salsa community mention the Turkish minority as problematic is particularly interesting because in none of the interviews did the interviewer mention this ethnic group. In contrast to people of Latin American origin, in the interviews the ethnic group of 'Turks' is described as unwilling to acquire German and is symbolic of the general undesired 'other'.[7] This seems to be an effect of national public discourse, as none of the interviewees base their claims on personal experience.

The salsa community produces exclusion not only with regard to the Turkish minority but also produces a negative image of Colombians. Yet, one respondent explicitly excuses Latin people's lack of German on the basis of class. An economically precarious situation here is an explanation for not succeeding in learning the language. Thus, this Colombian salsa dancer defends people with a Latin background who do not learn German on grounds of their difficult economic situation:

> Gente Latino que no aprende alemán,
> si hay (2)
> pero eso depende de la clase.
> Si uno no tiene educación y vive aquí feliz, no es grave. (1)
> Y también (.) tienen que trabajar tanto
> que no tienen tiempo para aprender el lenguaje. (J 33)
>
> Latin people who don't learn German
> yes, this happens (2)
> but this depends on class.
> If somebody has no education and lives here happily, it doesn't matter. (1)
> And also (.) these people have to work so much,
> they don't have time to learn the language.

The differentiation on the basis of class – 'eso depende de la clase' – is here only made for 'Latin' people. As has been observed by Collins and Slembrouck (2008: 5, 12), it is frequent not only in popular but also in academic and policy discourses in Europe to discuss deficit multilingualism in isolation from the effects of socio-economic background. As the interviewee is from Colombia, the exception that is made for Latin people can be interpreted as sympathy for those who are perceived as in-group members and who are known personally to the interviewee.

Generally, in the data set, language skills are problematised only with reference to people from economically marginal groups, while the 'authenticity' of those Latin Americans who have a leading role in the community, for example as dance teachers or DJs, is highly valued. It is interesting to note that in Sydney, ethnic segregation is also mentioned as a problem; however, it is here not linked to a lack of language skills (see the following two chapters). In Frankfurt, language ideological discourse from the national context is activated to legitimise social exclusion, which is, after all, exclusion based on a nexus of ethnicity *and* class, and not based on ethnicity or language competence alone.

To conclude this chapter, it can be first of all observed that the language discourse of Frankfurt salsa is characterised by a multiple interaction of discourses from different geographical scales and, at the same time, reproduces national concepts and discourses. For local native Germans, Spanish has functions of constructing an 'other' identity. This is based on a desire to get into contact with 'authentic' other cultures. This desire is interconnected with German imaginations of Latin Americans as emotional, warm and happy, which simultaneously, constructing a contrast to German 'coldness', indicates an awareness of the transnational gaze of the 'other'. Yet, a genuine belonging to 'other' cultures is seen as basically impossible; ethnic boundaries are seen as insurmountable. This parallels German public discourses, which are characterised by ethnic essentialisms. At the same time, ethnic boundaries are co-constructive of cosmopolitanism in Hannerz's sense. Cultural mobility indexes class identity, and in the form observed here, this mobility symbolically relies on the existence of ethnic and linguistic boundaries. Thus, ethnic boundaries do not necessarily blur in transnational culture: they may be necessary to develop a particular position in a transnational hierarchy. Similarly, boundaries between languages are not put into question.

Latin Americans generally enjoy a rather high status in the community on grounds of their ethnic authenticity – they are the 'real' ones. Dancers of other ethnic backgrounds sometimes exploit this by renegotiating their identity as 'Latin', as some ethnicities (particularly those associated with Islam) have a more negative image in public German discourses (and, in the case of Turkish, also in the discourses of the interviewees). This also indicates the (local/national) development of a transnational hierarchy. 'Other' ethnicities and languages are not generally regarded as a threat but are embedded in a hierarchical value scale, where Spanish and Latin American culture are locally valued because of their assumed 'otherness'. The positive value of this particular 'otherness' is linked to the history of Latin American–German relations and the transnational commercial success of music and other cultural products from Latin America.

Overall, the logic of linguistic capital (Bourdieu, 1980 [2005]) functions across cultural and linguistic boundaries and creates a complex local sociolinguistic economy. National ideals of a German-speaking population interact with hierarchies on the global scale and the outcomes are particular local discursive arrangements – in the case of Frankfurt salsa, German as 'norm', English as 'second language' that indexes education, and Turkish as 'lower class', whereas the functions of Spanish depend on the class and ethnic background of the speaker. A hierarchy of different languages and cultures is created at the intersection of local, national and transnational discourses. Languages are, similar to what has been described in relation to cultures (Appadurai, 1996: 60), no longer self-referential, in which case they would index ethnicity in a one-dimensional way. Here, indexical meanings of particular languages exist in interaction with those of other languages and their symbolic values. However, interestingly, the modernist concept of *language*, although it can be questioned theoretically and although it functions differently in transnational contexts, remains a vital concept in categorising the world. This relates to the fact that ethnic essentialism figures rather strongly in this German sample and demonstrates the continuing impact of national discourse on local environments.

It is enlightening to compare such observations with those from the Australian sample. Here, some informants explicitly mention competence and performance of an individual as more important than ethnic descent. On the other hand, neither ethnic nor linguistic boundaries become irrelevant in Sydney salsa. Again, it is the interaction of discourses from different contexts that makes local salsa communities in Sydney an intriguing example of the multiplexity of ideologies of language in an age of globalisation. Clearly, each salsa community comes into being as a 'knot' in a complex arrangement of transnational, national and local discourses and, like any other transnational community, the LA-style community in Sydney, presented in the following chapter, is also characterised by a complex layering of such local, national and global connections.

Notes

(1) Consider also the killings of Nationalsozialistischer Untergrund, a German terrorist group who killed nine people of non-German descent and one German police woman between 2000 and 2006. The killings were called *Dönermorde* (kebab killings) in official discourse and were attributed to the ethnic contexts of the victims, which is why they remained undiscovered for more than 10 years (see e.g. Ramelow, 2012).

(2) During my field visits, I only heard salsa songs with lyrics in Spanish but people reported to me that there are songs that are not in Spanish. Some Spanish (language) songs, however, have English words in them (for analyses of Salsa lyrics, see e.g. Aparicio, 1998; Hosokawa, 2002).

(3) Capital letters and numbers after quotes indicate the informant's first name (anonymised for reasons of privacy) and the minute of the interview from which the quote stems. See p. viii for transcription conventions.

(4) Shangri-La is a Tibetan utopia in James Hilton's 1933 novel *Lost Horizon*. The term is also used for describing other imagined ideal spaces, particularly those that represent retreats from the pressures of civilisation (Bishop, 1989).

(5) As I can personally attest from an experience in Australia during the period of research.

(6) The non-restrictive/restrictive distinction is not marked by a comma in German (a comma is always used). It is in any case impossible to conclude from the oral data whether this is a restrictive or non-restrictive clause.

(7) Although there were undoubtedly some Turkish dancers, it was not possible to estimate the ethnic composition of the salsa community (as indicated above).

5 'It Doesn't Matter What They Sing and How Sad They Are, They Always Sound Happy'. Evolutionist Monolingualism and Latin Branding in Sydney's LA-Style Salsa Community

Salsa practices in Sydney are rather different from the ones in Frankfurt (Box 5.1). There are several different and clearly separated communities constituted by salsa dance in Sydney, which is, above all, an effect of the size of the city (more than 4 million inhabitants). The different communities are mostly divided on the grounds of the salsa style practised. As my first experiences with salsa in Sydney were with LA-style salsa, and as the perspective from which I approached LA-style salsa in Sydney was influenced by my previous observations in Frankfurt, this book is structured according to the chronological order of my fieldwork, where I first observed salsa in Frankfurt (starting 2006) and then in Sydney (starting 2007). The most striking aspect of the LA-style community was that there were more or less no Spanish-speakers, either native or non-native. In order to understand the language ideologies of this environment, background knowledge is required, which I make available in the following.

I first talk about the societal discourses on language and multiculturalism in Australia. Secondly, I give some historical and ethnographic information on LA-style salsa in Sydney, which involves a closer look at the ethnic community of Colombians in Sydney, who were the first to bring salsa to the city. Thereafter, I present an analysis of the discourses on language as found in the LA-style salsa community, which leads to an analysis of discourses that are closely interwoven, namely ideas of commercialisation as cultural 'evolution' and the erasure of ethnicity for the sake of professional and capitalist development, tied to monocultural forms of globalisation and English monolingualism.

Box 5.1 Field note, 14 September 2007, Watershed Hotel

I sit on a bench at Darling Harbour and wait for my interview partner. It is already dark; we have an appointment at nine o'clock. Darling Harbour at night impresses me with all its lights that mirror in the water, with its many bars and restaurants and hotels. At the same time, I find it a very 'Disneyland'-like place. It is made for people to come to spend the night – and their money. The bar in which the salsa party takes place, where I will conduct my interview, is also very posh and bling-bling. It is certainly not a place where I would normally go to and it is very different from the places I have attended in Germany, with all its glitter, its bouncers, the red carpet and the ladies and men who look as if they would go to a prom. I am definitely under-dressed for the party later on. When my interview partner arrives, I am astonished by his white suit and business-like attitude.

Australian Public Discourses on Multiculturalism and Multilingualism

In official terms, Australia is a multicultural and multilingual nation and, since the 1970s, governmental bodies have engaged in a discourse of multiculturalism (Lopez, 2000). Overall, the country's history of multilingualism is diverse and sometimes contradictory. Despite a racist history with the White Australia Policy (implemented at the beginning of the 20th century – see Jayasuriya *et al.*, 2003), today, Australia belongs to one of the most ethnically diverse countries in the world. In 2006, according to the Australian Bureau of Statistics, 24% of the population of Australia was born overseas (see Australian Bureau of Statistics, 2007; Farrell, 2008: 24).

Australia was the first country to introduce a comprehensive programme to teach the national language to immigrants (Lo Bianco, 2003). In 1948, the AMEP, the Adult Migrant Education Program, was introduced (see Australian Government, Department of Immigration and Citizenship, 2009; McNamara & Shohamy, 2008), which was embedded in assimilationist policies until the 1970s. However, due to an increasingly diverse population in the 1960s, and the observation that assimilation policies led to segregation and poverty, in 1978, under the Liberal-National Fraser government, the Galbally report (Australian Government, 2009: 28; May, 2001: 182) implemented multiculturalism as an official policy. It was aimed at ensuring equal access to resources for all citizens and supported cultural maintenance (Jupp, 2001: 783). As a consequence, in the late 1970s and during the 1980s, Australia fostered a multicultural policy under which citizens were encouraged to reproduce their ethnic cultural heritage (Liddicoat, 2009; Lo Bianco, 2003). Local ethnic enclaves came into being; though no strict cultural divisions developed, there are suburbs of Sydney that were and still are known for their high number of residents from, for example, Italy, Greece, Portugal and so on.

Australia has been a crucial innovator in the field of inclusive language policies (see e.g. Lo Bianco, 2008; Ozolins, 1993; Phillipson & Skutnabb-Kangas, 1997). During the 1970s and 1980s, the interests of language professionals, community activists (indigenous and migrant) and of trade came together in a powerful coalition that made the language issue a national topic (Lo Bianco, 2001: 14). The results of activism for multilingual provision were unique and had a far reach. Languages spoken by the 'ethnic' (non-Anglo) communities in Australia became part of many primary schools' curricula (for a brief discussion of the different roles of 'community' and 'aboriginal' languages at that time, see Lo Bianco, 2003: 22). Radio programmes in community languages, interpreting in hospitals, provision of multilingual information leaflets in governmental institutions, telephone interpreting and multilingual television programmes belong to the crucial and outstanding innovations of language activism of the 1970s, and many of these remain in place today (Clyne, 2005: 145–151). In the second half of the 1980s, 'Australia became the first predominantly English-speaking nation to develop an explicit national languages policy. This has often been cited internationally as a model for pluralist language policy' (Clyne, 2005: 154). The National Policy on Languages (Lo Bianco & Australian Department of Education, 1987), also known as the Lo Bianco report, was introduced in 1987 and it 'stressed the importance of the recognition and promotion of languages other than English in the Australian context' (Kipp *et al.*, 1995: 20). As a consequence, in Europe, Australia is still perceived to be an innovator in the field of inclusive language policies (see e.g. Lo Bianco, 2003; Phillipson & Skutnabb-Kangas, 1997: 115).

Yet, it was merely four years after the Lo Bianco report, in 1991, that the policy was displaced by the Australian Language and Literacy Policy (ALLP). The emphasis shifted to literacy in English as 'economic rationalism became the dominant policy' (Clyne, 2005: 156). Its two foci are the learning of Asian languages and literacy in English, which are both related to a discourse of 'economic competitiveness in a global economy and an ideology of human capital theory' (Lo Bianco, 2003: 25–26). In 1997, the Commonwealth Literacy Policy (CLP) was introduced, which focuses exclusively on literacy in English. The 'CLP operates from assumptions of an English native speaking Australian community, almost a nostalgic recreation' (Lo Bianco, 2001: 34). The tendency to elevate 'the interests of economy above those of nation and community [...] constitutes a new kind of challenge for advocates of bilingualism and multilingual language planning' (Lo Bianco, 2003: 25). Australia thus represents an illustrative case for shifts from social to economic interests in national discourse (see also Lo Bianco, 2001), related to the globalisation of the economy, which at the same time normalises monocultural, monolingual tendencies with regard to English.

This also figures in the teaching of languages in Australian schools. Although many languages are accredited for examination (more than in any other country in the world, with over 40 languages accredited for examination at year 12 level – Lo Bianco, 2001: 40), Australia overall has a very limited provision of language learning. 'Australia's school students spend the least time on second languages of students in all OECD countries' (Lindsey, 2008). 'Other' languages are often understood as something that pertains to minority pupils only. The dominance of English is enforced by newly introduced language tests for migrants. Since 2007, new citizens have to attend a citizenship test, the test has to be taken in English and applicants have to demonstrate a 'basic knowledge of the English language' (Australian Citizenship Test Review Committee, 2008: 17). Concerning the visibility of multilingualism in the governmental sector, it is notable that multilingual service provisions of today's government web pages construct Australia as an English-speaking nation in which speakers of other languages may require help (other languages are used only where citizens need assistance – see e.g. http://australia.gov.au/topics/benefits-payments-and-services/multilingual-services-information).

In governmental discourse, speaking languages other than English remains tied to 1970s and 1980s discourses of cultural and linguistic diversity, where different cultures are supported for social reasons. It can be maintained that the construction of multilingualism in Australia intersects with marked ethnicity and lower-class identity, while English remains the 'normal' language. This contrasts with some semi-public sectors of Australian society, where a lively multilingual culture can be found. Thus, today, contradictory tendencies of economistic monolingualism and of pride in the multicultural composition of the country stand side by side in public discourses in Australia.

Ethnographic Observations on LA-Style Salsa in Sydney

Approaching salsa in Australia, it can first of all be observed that, similar to the German context, salsa is highly popular in urban areas. Salsa parties belong to the usual repertoire of nightlife in all major cities. Information on salsa parties, Latin bars and dance schools can be easily found in flyers and on the internet, for example. Looking at the history of salsa in Australia, according to my informants, today's presence of salsa in Australia is an effect of 1970s immigration from Latin America. In the case of Sydney, Colombians are mentioned as the first to bring salsa to the city. As discursive shifts from social to economic discourses become more accessible with an understanding of the role of Colombians in Sydney salsa contexts in the past and today, I will introduce some ethnographic observations on Colombian salsa first. For theoretical reasons (Colombians in Sydney do not form a salsa community of practice but an ethnic community) as well as practical reasons (the Colombian community mostly resides far away from the city centre, so that ethnographic fieldwork in these salsa venues was difficult to accomplish), Colombian salsa dancers who dance as part of their community activities were not focus of this study. However, I spoke to several individuals from this background, mainly at the *Latin Fiesta* that takes place annually at Darling Harbour at the centre of Sydney; I also conducted two more formal interviews with two women of Colombian background, as I was interested in their view on salsa in Sydney. The information collected for the following paragraphs is mainly based on these discussions, but partly also stems from interviews with dancers from the other salsa communities who had had early contacts with Colombians during the 1980s and 1990s.

Colombians arrived Sydney mostly on assisted migration schemes during the 1970s. Informants of mine who entered Australia in this way all spent their first months in so-called *migrant hostels*, where they received support from governmental agencies (see www.naa.gov.au/collection/fact-sheets/fs170.aspx). While dancing also belonged to the activities run by the hostels (and where, for example, one of my informants from the LA-style community of Filipino descent learned to dance salsa and to speak Spanish), people naturally also went out to get to know the city. According to my Colombian informants, some migrant hostels were in the centre of town and Latin dance bars were also established in central locations. As seems to be typical of the time, the Colombian women I spoke to had then moved to an area of Sydney where many Latin people lived and still do. This part of Sydney is called Fairfield and is located to the west, where housing is generally cheaper. Yet, they continued to go out in the city centre, mainly to a quarter of the city where there still are some Latin bars (the *Latin Quarter*), now primarily attended by tourists, and to a club at Circular Quay, which is now a posh nightclub that still offers some Latin dance nights.

The presence of Latin American people who actively practise their culture and dance has mainly shifted from the centre of the city to Fairfield. Latin American culture and language are more visible here: there are shops that sell food and other items from Latin America. Due to the early presence of Colombians, the main dance salsa style in the Latin communities is Colombian. Colombian-style salsa is characterised by its relative simplicity (Pietrobruno, 2006: 68). Typically, there are no courses for this style, and it is assumed that children learn to dance from their parents and other relatives and friends. This style is less elaborate than LA style and the main focus is on the experience of dancing as a couple. Couples are in a very close embrace (their bodies are in contact more or less from tip to toe) and the dance has, at least for an outsider, strong sexual connotations. In my data, dancers of this style have a positive attitude to the appropriation of 'their' cultural practice by others and see this as a sign of the attractiveness of their culture, although one informant notes that 'what the people do here is not salsa' (L 12).

It will become clearer in the following sections why Sydney Colombians sometimes do not regard as *salsa* the dance activities that take place in dance schools and in nightclubs in the centre of town today. In 2010, Colombian salsa became visible in the centre of town only during the aforementioned Latin Fiesta, which has a more folkoristic take on Latin American communities; otherwise, people interested in Colombian dance primarily meet at Marconi's (see www.clubmarconi.com.au). This is, actually, an Italian football club whose club house is located in Fairfield. Latin communities used the location to celebrate every fortnight, while nowadays Latin parties are offered on a regular basis, which, however, are no longer community events but are public parties. The relocation of 'ethnic' activities which take place in order to reproduce cultural heritage and to constitute as community (in contrast to activities whose main aim is financial profit), from the centre of town to its margins, and the merging of community activities from different ethnicities in the same places, is, considering price developments on the real estate market, not an accident and can certainly be observed in many other cities worldwide (thanks to Roxy Harris for alluding to this). This spatial distribution supports the discursive construction of the 'normal' Australian as Anglo-English-speaking, as opposed to 'traditional' and marginal speakers of heritage languages. Additionally, the shift from more socially oriented national discourses of the 1970s and 1980s to economistic national discourses from the 1990s and after may also have reinforced the perception of 'ethnic' identity as linked to the past. Keeping this in mind, it is fascinating to observe the activities, discourses and ideologies of LA-style salsa dancers today.

The fact that LA style is today widely danced in Sydney is an outcome of intercultural contact between Colombians and the owners of one of the dance schools that teach that style. The owners learned salsa from Colombians, who then still resided and danced in the town centre. Unsatisfied with the way Colombians taught the dance (focusing on imitation), the later owners of the dance school started to develop their own, more systemic way of teaching, influenced from their education in engineering and medicine (see also below). At a major inner-city festival in the late 1980s, the rum-producing company Barcadi sponsored the dance school to offer salsa courses for large groups during the festival, and, according to my informants, this is what 'made salsa big in Sydney' (V 7). LA-style salsa, in the period from 2007 to 2010, was the biggest and most visible community of practice in the city. Posters regarding the major events are found everywhere in central locations; it is easy to find dance schools of this type on the internet. Many lay dancers of LA style do not know that other styles of salsa exist, while dancers of other styles are very aware of this. This proves that LA style is the most dominant or 'unmarked' style in the city centre. As a result, this community is most likely to be the first one that an outsider gets into contact with – as happened in this study. Dancers of other styles comment frequently on the differences between styles, while dancers of LA style often do not mention other styles at all, or present them as 'out of date'. This construction of LA as norm and as being 'up to date' is important for understanding the discourses within the community and also connects to a particular language ideology, which will be discussed in more detail below.

As introduced above (see Chapter 3), the influence of ballroom dance is characteristic of LA style, which at the same time makes it more accessible to a Western public. While other salsa styles are characterised by far more body contact, couples who dance LA style usually do not touch each other's bodies: only their arms and hands get into contact. Because of the influence of ballroom dance, the steps and turns of LA style are relatively elaborate, complicated and technical. The style has a strong performance aspect, whereas other styles are usually not performed in front of an audience. This also makes LA style less an expression of popular culture and brings it closer to European 'high culture' and elite traditions of dance (Pietrobruno, 2006: 3). Local, national and global competitions are part of LA-style culture in Australia and being an elaborate, technically advanced dancer is an important cultural value.

Compared with the Frankfurt case, there is a notable absence of images that express 'Latin-ness' on posters and websites that relate to this community of practice. The biggest dance school, for example, Club Salsa, on its website refrains from images such as palm trees, palm leaves, sunsets, people with 'exotic' hairstyles, darker skin or flags from Latin American nations – images that are elsewhere typically associated with 'Latin' culture. Instead, an abstract symbol that represents fire and a dancing couple connect only in a very general sense to the cultural background of salsa. The visual style of Club Salsa is reminiscent of other popular mainstream music productions. In terms of the clothing of women and the colouring, it is especially contemporary RnB productions that share similar looks (e.g. Destiny's Child, Rihanna and the like). The presence of a *mission statement* on the website of the school is also striking, as it is a direct reference to business discourse.

LA-style parties are major events which take place in elaborate and expensive venues in the Central Business District of Sydney. The entrance fees for these parties are quite high (between A$15 and A$30 when the fieldwork was being conducted) – and the clothing is very elaborate. In general, LA-style salsa parties are characterised by expensive, stylish looks. As is common also in other party venues in Australia, many men wear suits and women usually wear evening gowns and jewellery – from a German perspective, dressed as for a ball. Based on experiences I had with salsa in Latin America and Australia alike, I assume this to be an effect of Australian standards rather than Latin American ones. The clothing at parties made this style less accessible to me, as I did not possess this type of outfit, which affected my ability to become a fully fledged member of these party events. It was therefore readily apparent that I was an outsider to this community. Nevertheless, attending these parties was not a negative experience, as the Australian public sphere generally has a very friendly and welcoming attitude. Although I felt like an outsider, I was asked to dance and was included in conversation. The majority of dancers in this context are white and Asian Australians. Their looks and attitudes can be considered white middle class and most interviewees and other informants worked in some kind of office, in banks, in insurance companies or advertising agencies.

Language in Sydney's LA-Style Salsa

The LA-style context is characterised by a stark absence of the Spanish language. It is in this sense comparable to other 'exotic' cultural practices that have been adapted to Western mainstream markets, for example yoga, kung fu or karate. While few people would describe it as remarkable that people who practise yoga do not speak Hindi or karatekas do not learn Japanese, the perception of an 'absence' of Spanish in this context is obviously based on my previous experiences in German contexts. Problematic issues with regard to the perspective taken in ethnographic research here come into play, as there is the danger, due to my German background, and because I had my first contact with salsa in Frankfurt, that I would construct Frankfurt salsa as 'normal' and LA-style salsa as deviant. Yet, it should be understood firstly that LA-style salsa in Sydney is just one potential relocation of salsa culture and secondly that relocation of salsa involves reconstructions of Latin culture and language in many other places, but does not do so here. Observations on LA-style salsa made below should not be understood as constructing it as a 'marked case'; nevertheless, it is unavoidable that I regard it as different from other salsa communities I know (because it clearly is). I consider the analysis of different discourses in different communities and their impact on language choice as highly illustrative and important in discussing the role of language in transnational culture, while I do not mean to say that any of the discourses is more legitimate than the others.

Interest in the Spanish language and in the culture of the places where salsa originates is very rare among LA-style dancers. The only display of Spanish words is on some posters or party flyers, where single words in Spanish occur, especially the term *fiesta* (party), although the terms of other Latin dances are kept in Spanish (merengue, bachata, both dances which are also popular with salsa dancers). Other than that, no usage of Spanish could be documented. In the dance classes that I attended, the instructions for the dance moves were in English. New moves were given English names. According to one dance instructor, this is because 'everybody can understand them' (K 38). Using Spanish names for dance moves is actually considered to be discriminatory, because, as the teacher adds: 'I don't want to come across as saying "you guys need to learn Spanish in order to learn salsa"' (K 39–40). English is thus seen as an inclusive tool, as enabling everybody to participate. While the songs that were played during the dance lessons and at parties always had Spanish lyrics, everything the dance teachers said was in English.

Initially, I was rather frustrated that the issue of learning and speaking Spanish, which had made salsa an attractive research choice for me in the first place, here seemed to be completely absent, as neither native nor non-native speakers of Spanish attended any of the classes or parties I went to. This absence seems to be related to the history of LA style in Sydney. Interestingly, the commercialisation of salsa here does not rely on the commodification of cultural authenticity, as is the case in many other salsa contexts; thus, 'nativeness' is not as much an issue. This has consequences for attitudes towards using, learning and speaking Spanish. The following section will introduce discourses of the community that pertain to language, while later sections will connect these to other discourses which I see as impacting on language choices in the community.

English Monolingualism and the Lack of 'Spanish People'

Looking more closely at the interview data with LA-style dancers, it becomes clear why the Spanish language is never used and has no prestige in the community. Besides the role of English in global dance competitions, where English is used as the lingua franca, a particular discourse on cultural 'evolution' seems to be responsible for a lack of interest in Spanish and a clear English monolingual ideology.

Based on my fieldwork in Frankfurt, I included a question on language choice in my interviews with informants from LA-style salsa. Most of my informants were puzzled when I asked about the role of Spanish in the community and seemed to consider the question to be inappropriate, which is why the topic was typically not contemplated in length in interviews. Interviewees did not see a point in speaking or learning Spanish, as nobody did so in their social environment. The most common reason that was mentioned for a potential usefulness of Spanish is the ability to understand the lyrics of the songs. But then, as is assumed by a dance instructor:

> They [the songs] all only deal with love anyways,
> it's pretty boring. (V 1.16)

Due to the predominant interest in the dance steps and the performance of the dance, the music and its cultural background are not of interest for LA-style dancers. Thus, stereotypical assumptions about Latin culture guide the interpretation of song lyrics. They 'deal with love' and there is nothing interesting about that. The effort of learning Spanish is, consequently, avoided, which is reinforced by the fact that native Spanish-speakers do not usually attend the places where LA style is danced:

> Spanish doesn't really come into it.
> I don't speak Spanish.
> [X][1] doesn't speak Spanish.
> [Y] doesn't speak Spanish (2).
> Uhm (1) but the lack of Spanish makes no difference whatsoever.
> 'Cause we don't actually deal with the Spanish people. (J 7)

For this interviewee, speaking Spanish would be of interest only if the community would encompass people who actually speak Spanish. As in some other quotes, the interviewee does not differentiate between people from Spain and people from Latin America and thus constructs a rather broad category of 'Spanish' 'others'.

Despite an overall striking absence of people of Latin American heritage in the community, some dance teachers mention that, however, there are some Latin Americans who do learn to dance LA style. The following quote, an interview conversation passage between me (B) and a female dance teacher of Hungarian descent (V), not only shows that the fact that Latin people learn to dance LA style is conceptualised as 'evolution' but furthermore shows that this evolutionist discourse is related to the acquisition of English:

V: And they [the Latin Americans] have started coming in and started to evolve it as well.
So I mean, there's more Spanish people coming in.
B: But they are like everybody else¿
V: Just like everybody else.
I mean. They (2)
so I mean, somebody's got to lead.
And maybe it's not always the people from Latin culture who lead.
B: Yeah. (.) Yeah.
V: <u>Bút.</u> It's, you know.
Basically, it's a wake-up call.
It really is a wake-up call.
To the origins of Latin culture, to get them all off to learn English, not left behind.
It's hilarious to see
and I still see a lot of (envy¿)
from some of the people from Latin culture. (V 1.21)

The English language is here directly related to a discourse on cultural 'evolution' into the more 'mainstream' (commercialist, 'white') culture of LA-style salsa. Learning English and dancing LA style are both embedded in this discursive construction that relates to time. Latin people (here also referred to as 'Spanish') 'evolve' when they 'wake up' and learn English; they should not be 'left behind'. The 'origins of Latin culture' are conceptualised as being 'behind' and this construction here relates to time: they are seen as remaining in the past.

Latin people seem to need somebody who 'gets them all off to learn English'. The interviewee also expresses her supportive attitude by saying that Latin people should not be 'left behind' (maybe also an intertextual reference to the No Child Left Behind Act introduced in the US in 2001, which is concerned with improving public education – see US Department of Education, 2001); somebody has to help them to 'evolve'. As can be inferred, those who help Latin people to 'evolve' are those who are 'leading'. Competitive and hierarchical discourses are adopted and projected onto salsa dance ('I mean, somebody's got to lead') and in the case of LA-style salsa, it is, obviously, not the 'people from Latin culture' who lead. The fact that salsa – which is tacitly still attributed to Latin culture – is now 'led' by non-Latins in this community is nevertheless perceived as 'hilarious'. Although it is explained that Latin people have not evolved sufficiently and that others now lead, this is still considered, in a way, to be unusual. It is 'hilarious' that Latin culture now has to be taught by others, as Latins somehow have stuck in the past. The perception of Latin people as remaining in the past is confirmed by the observation that they 'still' envy the non-Latin leaders but the adjective 'still' perhaps implies that, if the evolution goes on, they will eventually also understand that competitive white middle-class culture, LA-style salsa and speaking English are 'more evolved' forms of behaviour.

It has been observed that ethno-symbolism, English as signifying British or American culture, is usually not present if English is used to promote goods on non-English markets (Androutsopoulos, 2007: 221). English is here used to indicate novelty, modernity, internationalism, hedonism, fun and so on. The construction of English as 'modern' or 'up to date' is also detectable in the above quote, where English is not directly described in its function as an ethnic signifier but as tied to the discourse of cultural 'evolution' that exists within this salsa context, which, at the same time, is also found in Australian national discourse on the integration of migrants, above all, before the 1970s and after the 1980s.

The construction of an 'evolution' is found not only with regard to language but also with reference to other cultural traits, as discussed below. An attitude that considers Latin people to be relatively simple-minded or 'under-developed' (e.g. being interested only in love) can also be detected in the community's discourses on the music and its lyrics, which, according to the following quote, 'always sound happy', even if the contents are sad:

> If you're listening to salsa music, they might be singing
> 'oh, I'm so sad, my girlfriend has dumped me, I just lost my house, I live on the streets'
> and you listen to it and it sounds so happy.

> The music sounds <u>sóooo</u> just like having a party.
> It doesn't matter what they sing and how sad they are,
> they always sound happy, and happy and exciting. (B 10)

Although this interviewee is aware that many songs have a sad or even tragic content, the important point for him is not what the musicians of salsa songs want to express but that (for him) the songs always sound 'happy and exciting'. Obviously, for somebody who speaks Spanish, the songs will not always sound happy and exciting, as, indeed, many songs have the topic of unanswered love or, especially older songs, as has been introduced in Chapter 3, have a strong political message. For the informant, this is irrelevant, as the focus is on the general, stereotypical perception that salsa music is 'like having a party' (B 11).

While Spanish and Spanish-speakers are almost denigrated in the above quotes, English is tied to an evolutionist, capitalist-competitive discourse. Similar to some public discourses in Australia, multilingualism is constructed as irrelevant. Being an English-speaker is one aspect of becoming a member of the 'normal' local LA-style community. On the other hand, the LA-style community is also part of a transnational community and, on a transnational level, as in international competitions, it also makes use of English. English serves as tool of communication among people of different language backgrounds, in local and global contexts alike. So, by acquiring the English language and LA-style dancing skills, Latin Americans (and all others) can, simultaneously, become part of the Australian mainstream culture and members of an English-speaking competitive culture, where ethnic identity and other languages than English are considered a thing of the past. At the same time, this discourse has very inclusive aspects, as the majority of informants with whom I spoke did not speak English as a first language, but non-native accents in English were never regarded as a problem.

Yet, the discourse of LA-style salsa as 'developed' hides the fact that Latin Americans may dance differently but do not necessarily aim at 'developing' towards mainstream culture. It is very likely that the absence of Latin Americans and of the Spanish language in the community is related to the perception of Latin people as overly traditional, 'undeveloped' and as somehow 'in the past'. Indeed, it seems that this construction deters Latin Americans from participating in the community and may even reinforce their desire to maintain their own style of dancing, which is referred to as 'backyard salsa' (V 21) several times in interviews with LA-style dance teachers. It is also mentioned that Colombians' way of dancing 'hasn't developed since the 1970s' (V 25). Thus, the dichotomy of Latin as stuck in the past and of English as an endpoint of an evolution can be found not only with regard to language, but also with reference to dance style. Therefore, instead of celebrating Latin Americans for their presumed 'authenticity', as is done in Frankfurt salsa, they are described as being unable to dance:

> If you're a Latin American [in Sydney], you, (¿)
> they just have a great time,
> they move to the rhythm,
> the whole body moves but they dance two turns and (movey¿) and stuff,
> they don't do ever a (shine[2]¿)
> they wanna dance, but you know,
> they cán't. (J 10)

This quote lists the presumed behavioural features of Latin Americans on LA-style dance floors and thus has an almost 'scientific' approach to observing the 'others', who are again presented in stereotypical forms that almost reminiscent of colonial racism ('they just have a great time', 'the whole body moves'), while their assumed essential inability to dance is focused on ('they wanna dance, but you know, they can't').

The construction of an evolutionist scale of culture, language and dance that we have seen in this section can be attributed to two related discourses. One is concerned with a commercialist and technical approach to the cultural practice of dancing, the other with how multiculturalism and cosmopolitanism are conceptualised in the community. Although these discourses make no direct reference to language, it is important to consider these as co-responsible for the symbolic meaning of English as 'norm' and as 'developed' on a national and on a transnational scale.

Systematising and Commercialising Salsa Steps

The evaluation of Latin American ways of dancing as a thing of the 1970s and of non-English cultures and languages as being behind is, besides the clear links to national discourses of the integration of migrants and the dominance of English in global spheres, also embedded in very local histories. Yet, in these local histories, global discourses of capitalism, commerce and a single 'world culture' become visible. Starting on local grounds, it has been elaborated above that Colombian migrants brought salsa to Sydney and that two dance school owners, who are now central figures in the LA-style community, learned to dance salsa from Colombians. The move from Colombian-style salsa to how salsa is taught, learned and practised today in Sydney's LA style did not go without tensions, as indicated in the following quote from an interview I led with an LA-style dance teacher rather informally in a café, aiming to know more about the history of salsa in Sydney:

> [X] and [Y] had a falling out with [Z]
> because [X] and [Y] wanted to take it big. (3)
> Mainstream.
> They wanted to make it public, they wanted everybody to know it.
> The rest of the committee was very apprehensive.
> [X] and [Y] decided
> 'Oh, we gonna do this on our own.
> We gonna do this regardless.' (V 10)

Although ethnicity is not explicitly mentioned in this quote, the intention to take salsa 'mainstream' implies – in the context of the historical development of salsa in Sydney, where only Latin people would dance salsa until the middle of the 1980s – a move away from the ethnic symbolism of the dance. The interviewee presents X and Y as very active, in contrast to the other, 'apprehensive' members of the 'committee', who were Colombians who had come together to discuss the future of salsa in Sydney (unfortunately, the interviewee did not give more information on this event or what the 'committee' was about). In any case, a positive attitude towards the distribution of salsa to a mainstream audience in this case implies a general positive evaluation of the transformation of cultural forms into 'mass products' (the usage of a business term like 'committee' may thus be explainable). Commodification of salsa and inter-ethnic struggles are here clearly linked. This becomes clear also with regard to how dance steps are analysed and taught differently by 'native' and 'non-native' dancers of salsa.

In the following quote, one of the dance school owners mentioned above assumes that a lack of analytical skills is responsible for the lack of Latin people in the LA-style community and for their inability to profit commercially from the dance. He (himself of Chinese descent[3]) explains how he learned to dance from Colombians in Sydney and then comments on their lack of professionalism:

> Before that, all the things (0.5)
> they wére pássionate,
> and they were very very strong about their culture and everything (0.5)
> but they were not very (1) technicál.
> And when we went and asked them,
> they said,

> 'ah, follow your heart, follow the music'
> and we got soo frustrated.
> We said 'so how do you do the steps¿'
> and they couldn't really break it down (1)
> they're not very technical. (B 10)

The informant criticises Latin American salsa dancers, who obviously assume that dancing is learned by imitation – which is how it is done in Colombia. The informant admits that 'they' (he did not specify exactly whom he was referring to) consider their culture to be important but fail to transmit their knowledge to others in an understandable way. It is especially the lack of a systematic analysis of the dance steps that the informant criticises, as outsiders are thereby hindered in learning the dance. The rising tone at the end of line 4, making the passage sound like a question, is a typical Australian intonation, termed a high rise terminal (HRT), in narrative talk (see e.g. Holmes, 2008: 210). The long pause before the word 'technical' can be interpreted as an expression of a critical stance that is taken towards Latin American salsa dancers who simply engage in dancing but cannot explain verbally how they do it. This is again mentioned at the end of the passage, where the informant concludes that 'they' are not technical, this time using the present tense, making the essentialist claim even stronger.[4]

As a consequence of the felt need for a more systematic approach to teaching, the above interviewee and his 'business partner' – a friend whom he met when learning salsa – not only analysed the dance steps, but furthermore broke down whole movements into smaller sections, before they developed a method of teaching these steps, implementing several 'levels' according to which their dance classes are structured. The informant explains that

> Because I am a doctor by training and my business partner engineer,
> so we are very analytical,
> so we analysed all the steps and that's how we (made it¿)
> so we are very methodical, systematic and that's the main reason
> we, our (thing¿) was a big hit. (B 15)

While the commercial interests of dance schools and sponsors were described as the underlying cause for the success of salsa at the beginning of the interview, the reason why this particular dance school became so successful is seen in the analytical approach to the teaching of dancing. It is later explicitly referenced to undergraduate textbooks that the two founders of the school used during university studies in engineering and medicine, where information is presented in an orderly, systematic fashion, and that served as an inspiration for appropriating salsa.

Overall, there are interesting inter-discursive references here. The approach taken towards salsa dancing is obviously a projection from types of knowledge acquired in business and university contexts. The way they structure and teach salsa is explicitly taken from these contexts and thus the informant calls his school a 'business' and also mentions his 'business plan', and that the school is 'a corporate thing'. The informant is proud of his ability to make money with salsa and does not conceal his commercial interests. Presumably, this is also an effect of Australian discourses on commercialism, as it would be almost unthinkable to detect such open references to business in German salsa contexts, where commercialism is regarded in more negative terms (although, of course, German salsa schools are also commercial actors).

The following quote confirms a strong tendency to regard salsa in terms of capitalist business discourse in LA-style salsa. When asked about what he believes to be the reasons for salsa being a success on a global level, the informant maintains that it is because it is something that is easy to make money with. He then says:

> Well, I think, any kind of dancing is attractive.
> To a lot of people. (1)
> Many venues opened, many dance schools. (2)
> You need the packages.
> You need a good product. (1)
> All that you learn from business management, you know,
> customer relations, management,
> they are all the same, there is no difference. (B 23)

The inter-discursive references to business discourse are again very obvious in this quote: 'packages' are usually sold by banks (e.g. *investment packages*) or in tourism (*all-inclusive packages*). A 'product' is commonly defined by its quality of being manufactured for sale. In the last two lines, the interviewee maintains that because of the good quality of the 'product' salsa, he just had to apply general knowledge from business contexts – 'customer relations', 'management' – and thus made his school financially profitable and salsa popular. Salsa dance, for this interviewee, is embedded in a discourse that belongs to a capitalist business sphere. This capitalist discourse can be considered to be related to a global scale, as this is the dominant financial system worldwide (with the exception of Cuba, where, paradoxically, salsa's ancestors stem from). Salsa here has been moved from the realm of a cultural practice that was originally tied to a political discourse, and to the expression of cultural identity, to the sphere of capitalist exploitation. The move between different discourses is described as 'common-sense', as it seems obvious to the interviewee that 'You need a good product'. A business attitude towards salsa is portrayed as positive, and it is normalised through the uncommented construction of salsa as 'product'. Although any popular music production is tied to the capitalist market, and although, as has been mentioned above, salsa has been embedded into this system right from its beginnings, it still struck me as unusual that the commercialisation of culture is not hidden or legitimised, as is often the case in other contexts of music culture, where 'resistance' to systems of exploitation are important elements in marketing strategies.

LA-style salsa in Sydney has moved away from ethnic roots – the culture of Latin America is not part of the 'package' – whereas in other salsa contexts, it is exactly these roots that are adhered to and which are also sold. Interestingly, the commercialisation and systematisation of salsa is regarded as culturally 'neutral' and never mentioned as something 'Australian' (or maybe US-American). The erasure of ethnicity in competitive, capitalist discourses is here indirectly linked to English monolingualism. This can also be inferred from the community's ideologies with regard to multiculturalism and their construction of cosmopolitanism, which is rather different from Hannerz's definition (see Chapter 2).

Erasures of Ethnicity – Culturally 'Neutral' Cosmopolitanism

Because of the lack of both Latin Americans and the Spanish language in this community, I asked my interviewees about the ethnic composition of the community. Interviewees usually highlighted that salsa is for everybody, irrespective of ethnic descent. It is, for example, explained that

> It's a hub for people for all nationalities,
> they basically came from all over the place.
> You have people from South America, from North America,
> you have people from Europe,
> you have people from the Pacific,
> you have people from (Asia¿),
> So, and we all came together
> and everybody is so different into it. (V 16–17)

The absence of Latin people in this salsa community seems to go unnoticed in this quote (indeed, there is a rather blithe claim that 'You have people from South America'). It is common in the LA context to describe salsa as an activity that stands out for its ethnic inclusion. The inclusion of all ethnic backgrounds is something that is mentioned often and is evaluated positively by all interviewees. In the quote above, it is furthermore stated that 'everybody is so different into it', expressing a positive attitude towards diversity itself. This appraisal of diversity and ethnic mixing can be set in relation to Australian discourses on ethnic inclusion, where official discourses continuously emphasise the fact that Australia is a culturally diverse nation (see above). The inclusion along ethnic lines is found among salsa professionals as well as among students of LA style, as one owner of a dance school notes:

> My business partner, he's Italian.
> And, uhm, my instructor, she's Hungarian.
> We come from so many different backgrounds.
> In my team, we have people from all around the world.
> My customers, come from all over, you know. (B 30)

There is a strong emphasis on ethnic inclusion and, paradoxically, this almost implies a refusal of people who are 'really' of Latin descent, who, because of their 'authentic' background do not fit into the framework of inclusion as promoted here. In line with an ideology of ethnic inclusion, interviewees strongly oppose the view that authentic ethnic descent is a valuable resource in salsa. One dance teacher (of Arab descent) illustrates that he thinks that Latin heritage is unnecessary when dancing and teaching salsa:

> I mean, you don't need to be Italian to make a good pizza.
> You see, you don't need to be from China to cook some noodles.
> You don't <u>need</u> to have that background. (K 24)

The interviewee places a strong emphasis on the irrelevance of ethnic descent. Although I never argued that being Latin is a precondition for dancing salsa, when asked about the situation of Latin people in the community, interviewees from this community explained that ethnic authenticity does not play any role at all. The emotionality with which a relevance of ethnic authenticity is denied, also shared in some of the quotes of other interviewees, suggests that some, particularly teachers, may have been criticised for not being Latin.

Considering the ethnically very diverse LA-style community, it does not come as a surprise that social inclusion and success are not linked to ethnic descent. Similar to what Australian national discourse constructs – being Australian is based on values and performance, not on ethnicity (consider also Australian visa laws that put educational background and financial capital at the foreground – see Australian Government, Department of Immigration and Citizenship, 2010) – LA-style dancers refuse ethnicity as a cultural value. This comes along with a particular conceptualisation of 'cosmopolitanism', which is different from the concepts of cosmopolitanism introduced above. In the following quote, the interviewee considers the local environment – Sydney – as 'cosmopolitan', an attitude that he distinguishes from a 'mentality of heritage, of ethnic heritage':

> So Sydney is such a melting pot.
> So cosmopolitan.
> I give you an example,
> the girls here come from all over the world.
> So we are all international,
> we are all universal in many ways.
> I think mentality of heritage, of ethnic heritage, cultural heritage is very narrow minded. (B 33)

Next to the sexist implications of this quote (on gender and heteronormativity in salsa, see Schneider, 2013a, 2013b), it is intriguing to observe that ethnic and cultural heritage are not valued positively but seen as 'narrow minded'. The construction of 'cosmopolitanism' is here linked to a concept of culture where ethnicity and heritage are erased for the sake of a 'universal', commercial and competitive culture. This particular understanding of cosmopolitanism is different from cosmopolitanism as it is found in cultural anthropological literature (Chapter 2; Hannerz, 1996a) or in dictionary definitions, where it is reads as 'familiar with and at ease in many different countries and cultures' (*New Oxford American Dictionary*, 2009). In this understanding of cosmopolitanism, it does denote that people from different cultural backgrounds participate but that these 'international' people do not reproduce different cultures but are supposed to take part in a 'universal' culture. From what one can gather from the quote, it is Anglo-Australian commercial culture that is considered 'cosmopolitan' as it accepts the participation of people of other ethnic backgrounds.

Interestingly, Ulf Hannerz also mentions the case of people who are in contact with people from other cultures but are not interested in acquiring competence in other cultures. He considers these to be 'metropolitan locals' (Hannerz, 1996a: 107). Hannerz assumes that it is mainly people from Western backgrounds who become 'metropolitan locals', as most transnational cultures are 'extensions' of the cultures of Europe and North America. '[W]estern Europeans and North Americans can encapsulate themselves culturally, and basically remain metropolitan locals instead of becoming cosmopolitans' (Hannerz, 1996a: 107). Discourses on ethnicity in LA-style salsa in Sydney thus appropriate a Latin American cultural practice according to Anglo-Western values of achievement and competition. 'Cosmopolitan' here does not mean interaction between different cultures but interaction between people with the same values and discourses, irrespective of their ethnic background. One might interpret this as a form of erasure of ethnicity in global capitalist regimes (in contrast to erasures of ethnicity in national regimes; see Irvine & Gal, 2000), which may be accused of invisibilising culture but, in their focus on commercial and technical performance, are indeed inclusive in ethnic terms – which can also be inferred from the fact that most of the above speakers are not 'Western' in a traditional sense.

Interestingly, the quality of being 'Latin' is not rejected as value when it comes to products (music and dance) and not people. In explaining why salsa, although danced, taught and distributed in Australia by people who are not Latin, still remains very 'Latin', it is claimed:

> You can still (2)
> even if you (3)
> you can still feel the rhythm, you can, (0.5)
> it is <u>sooo</u> Latin, you know. (B 17)

The long pauses in this quote show that the interviewee has difficulties to express his view and the quote remains, content-wise, very vague, as a circular argument is produced by saying that something is 'Latin' because it is 'Latin'. When I ask what exactly he means by something being 'Latin', quite unexpectedly, the previously very rational, business-minded dance school owner argues that

> It's something that you feel in your heart. (B 18)

The quality of being 'Latin' is here constructed as an essence that simply has to be 'felt'. A discourse based on emotionality, although absent in the explanations of the commercialisation of salsa, is adhered to. Paradoxically, anything 'Latin' is rejected as irrelevant if it relates to people ('you don't need to be Italian to make a good pizza') but it is appreciated when it comes to the 'product'. This connects these micro-level discourses to broader discourses on globalisation, where it is frequently noted that globalisation enables the flow of capital and goods but restricts the flow of (particular) human beings — for example, through tighter migration and naturalisation regimes (see e.g. Solimano & Watts, 2005).

Summarising this chapter, we can see that the above discourses of commercialism and culturally 'neutral' cosmopolitanism interestingly link to the ideologies of language in the community. English is the 'unmarked' and invisible norm and medium of communication. The usage of English does not index ethnic identity, but seems more tied to an evolutionist discourse of capitalism, and, at the same time, national inclusion and international communication. 'The world language par excellence is English, and in many parts of the world, English is indeed semiotized as being the emblem of international mobility, success, and prosperity' (Blommaert, 2007: 13). Yet, the focus on commercial ideology and success, to which the English language is tied, is not a racist discourse; rather, social hierarchies are built on the ability to adopt competitive values and to perform. Spanish, on the other hand, is heard in the music, and some words and sentences are found on material products such as flyers or posters. Spanish functions more like a brand. Words and expressions like *fiesta* or *una noche de salsa* convey 'the Latin touch' and this 'exploits the symbolic rather than the referential, functions of language' (Androutsopoulos, 2007: 214). Overall, in the language ideologies of the LA-style community, English is for everybody, completely normalised and does not express ethnic belonging, while Spanish serves for branding the salsa product as 'Latin'. Such language ideologies may be taken as indicative of global regimes of power beyond nationalism. It should be finally noted that the many native languages of Australia remain invisible, as well as the fact that most of the members of this community of practice are actually bi- or multilingual.

In discussing the second research question – which discourses co-construct local language ideologies – it has been shown that, similar to observations in Frankfurt, language ideologies are tied to discourses from several geographical scales at the same time. On the local level, lack of interest in the Spanish language is related to the desire to differentiate from 'ethnic' cultures, which implies interesting constructions of time in which 'ethnic' culture is perceived as belonging to the past. 'Ethnic' communities also reside in more marginal places in the city; thus there are interlocked aspects of time and space. Simultaneously, the use of English expresses 'normal', middle-class Australian (national) identity and ideologies of ethnic inclusiveness, which also can be attributed to the national scale. Understanding 'ethnic' culture as related to a time in the past is also linked to Australian policy discourse, where the celebration of multiculturalism was important in 1970s and 1980s social discourses (see above; and Lo Bianco, 2001). Finally, English expresses belonging to a transnational sphere. This transnational scale is characterised by commercialist discourse and globalised capitalism, and the construction of monocultural cosmopolitanism ('metropolitan localism') to which the English language is connected (for further discussion on this connection, see e.g. Piller, 2010a). Thus, in the case of LA-style salsa in Sydney, the local, the national and the transnational scale all co-construct and mutually strengthen the construction of English as a 'normal', 'up-to-date' medium of communication that is associated with positive images of success.

Relating this to the question of the role of the discursive construction *language*, it can, first of all, be noted that the deconstruction of reified notions of language as constructed in a national era is not relevant in this environment. English is seen as an entity, a 'normalised' medium of communication, while Spanish is also seen as an entity but related to 'other' people, places and times. It is only the use of Spanish as 'branding' the activities of the community as 'exotic' and 'Latin' that shows a certain disentanglement of language from ethnicity. Spanish on LA-style marketing items does not necessarily make reference to ethnicity but, instead, to a commodified form of lively, exotic and happy party times. In this sense, we can detect language use that questions national language ideology, as a language is here no longer related to a group. However, members of the community show no signs of a discourse that would question the perception of language as coming into being in the form of bounded, static systems that basically express ethnic difference. The perception of English as a medium of communication, and of other languages as a supplement for marketing strategies or for purely private realms, is somewhat reminiscent of pre-modern times, when Latin was considered the only 'real' language, and all other forms of verbal expression were deemed 'vulgar' (see e.g. Arens, 1969: 56).

Ideologies of language are deeply embedded in other discourses on culture and community. An interesting finding is that the symbolic functions of language in this transnational context seem less tied to spatial or political entities (countries, regions, etc.) but more to capitalist ideology and constructions of time, where the figure of 'evolution' constructs English as being related to the highest rank within this 'evolution'. Accordingly, ideologies of language, identity and time intersect strongly with social hierarchies. We have already seen that the development of meaning is a very local matter and, as it depends on the specific discursive arrangement in different localities, is accessible only in local terms. In the following chapter, I introduce another salsa community that is found in Sydney, which, interestingly, has developed fairly different discourses on culture, dance and language.

Notes

(1) X and Y substitute for the first names of two central figures in the community.
(2) A *shine* is a combination of steps that is danced without the partner.
(3) I mention the ethnic backgrounds of interviewees here as I see this as relevant in accessing the community's discourses on ethnicity.
(4) The same line of argument is also found on the school's website.

6 'It's Also the Cool Factor'. Multilingualism and Authenticity in Sydney's Cuban-Style Salsa Community

Compared with LA-style salsa, in Sydney's Cuban-style community we find a different world of salsa, embedded in different discourses on culture, language and authenticity (Box 6.1). It has been mentioned (Chapter 3) that this is indexically tied to the dance style itself. While LA style concentrates on intricate foot choreographies and showy dance moves, Cuban style focuses on the movements of the body as a whole; 'holistic body movements', as a teacher of this style describes it, are considered important, and more individual variation is possible (see Chapters 3 and 5). It is fascinating to observe that a discourse that expresses access to the 'real thing' and that partly rejects competitive commercialist values is not only displayed in verbal contents of utterances but is also found in

Box 6.1 Field note, 24 September 2007, Salsa Republic

It is not too easy to find the Cuban-style dance school, as it is located in a little shabby lane close to the railway station. From the outside, it does not look like a dance studio but more like an old, no longer used warehouse. There is a sign on the door, made from cardboard, where someone wrote down the name of the school. When I enter the dance school, I am surprised how bright it is from the inside, as it all looked so gloomy from the outside. My informant is giving a private dance lesson, so I sit down on an old sofa next to the entrance and watch the lesson for a while. It is nice to sit here and listen to the music and watch the dance, while the morning sun is shining through the roof-lights. Finally, my interview partner welcomes me and greets me with kisses on the cheeks. With her long hair and colourful dress, and with her whole way of talking and moving, she makes a very lively and also a bit of an artsy impression but I think that it is nice to see someone who seems to have made a living from a real passion.

the choice of locations, in room decoration, in clothing, ways of talking and, furthermore, is co-constituted by how dance moves are interpreted (on multimodality, although mostly concerned with visual expression, see Kress & Leeuwen, 2001). Sydney's Cuban-style salsa, in its construction of the cultural 'other' as a value, has strong similarities to salsa in Frankfurt, while there are, obviously, also differences. Comparing the constructions in this context with the ones in another country (Frankfurt), and with those of an ideologically very different but nonetheless local background (LA style), is a highly enlightening enterprise to illustrate different trajectories of discourses in motion in an age of globalisation. And despite all their differences, all communities demonstrate impacts of economic discourses and of the formation of transnational class structures.

In this chapter, I first introduce ethnographic observations on the community. I will not discuss Australian public discourse anew, neither will I include in this chapter the background history of salsa in Sydney as based on Colombian's dance practices. The reader is referred to the previous chapter, as the information given here pertains to both LA and Cuban styles. I do discuss the community's language ideologies and demonstrate their links to a discursive complex of anti-commercialism, cosmopolitanism (as discussed by Hannerz – see Chapter 2) and the development of class at the intersection of national and transnational discourses.

Ethnographic Observations

At the time of my research, there were only two schools in Sydney that taught Cuban-style salsa and one of these schools is here described as the centre of the Cuban-style community.[1] Even so, although most of that school's classes were in Cuban style, it did also teach LA style. As Cuban-style dancers typically have a rather negative attitude towards LA style, it can be assumed that the inclusion of LA-style lessons was largely on economic grounds, LA style being much more popular than Cuban style in Sydney and so offering a larger number of potential students. At first, I was not aware of the sometimes very strong ideological differences and also animosities between Cuban-style and LA-style dancers. It is thus safe to say that the distinctions between the two discourses, LA versus Cuban, are not based on my own pre-assumptions or potential suggestive questions in the fieldwork or in interviews.

The Cuban-style dancers can be described as a 'minority' or 'marked' salsa community, in contrast to the LA-style community. This can be inferred from the fact that most lay LA-style dancers, as I mentioned in Chapter 5, do not know that there are different styles of salsa, whereas

Figure 6.1 Logo of the Salsa Republic dance school, from its website, www.salsarepublic.com.au, 18 September 2013 (note that the star is coloured red in the original image)

Cuban-style dancers, even those who do it just for fun, are very aware of LA-style salsa and usually produce a strong construction of difference with regard to this other community. Professional LA-style dancers do know that different styles exist. It was the LA-style teacher of Hungarian descent, some of whose quotes were discussed in Chapter 5, who referred me to the owner of the Cuban-style dance school when I asked about people who dance salsa and speak Spanish. Also, on the professional level, there are contacts across styles, especially at public events like the Latin Fiesta or at accidental meetings at large concerts by famous Latin American salsa bands. Nevertheless, it has to be noted that lay dancers from my data set usually do not mix with other salsa communities, and the places where Cuban-style dancers go are very different from the ones that LA-style dancers attend.

Although I had heard already about the existence of the Cuban-style school from my LA-style dance teacher interviewee, my first tangible contact with it came about through a tiny flyer that was attached to a signpost, close to Sydney's Central Railway Station. As the field note above introduces, the dance studio is located in a loft in a small dark street close to where I found the flyer. The area is a poor neighbourhood that is in the process of being gentrified due to its central location. It is typical of a trendy, bourgeois area inhabited by less wealthy people, by students, artists and intellectuals. The atmosphere of the school provokes stereotypical images of poor but passionate dancers in Hollywood movies such as *Flashdance*. The logo of the school, a red star, is a reminder of the origins of Cuban-style salsa and of Cuba's communist regime (Figure 6.1). The first impression of the school confirms the fact that salsa dancing is here related to very different ideologies than what has been documented in the LA-style environment.

Concerning the outward appearance of dancers, there are obvious differences between LA-style and Cuban-style salsa. Clothing is much more casual in the Cuban community than in the LA community. The dressy style of the LA-style dancers contrasts with the jeans and t-shirts typically worn in the Cuban-style context. The casual clothing, the slightly shabby impression of the location and the red stars that are found on flyers and posters in connection with the interest in Cuban dance produce a different atmosphere and are linked to what I would call a left-wing discourse, where people have a more critical stance towards commercialism or may be interested in 'alternative' lifestyles. Politically liberal ideologies are approached with a positive attitude; in the context of Australia, this typically means a strong adherence to multiculturalism. Some interviewees explicitly refer to the political meanings of Cuban style (see also the final section of this chapter). The impression that more 'left-wing', less commercial ideologies are appreciated in this environment also relies on observations regarding the decoration in places where the style is danced. The dance school's shabby looks have already been mentioned; the bar where the school's parties are held is a normal pub, decorated with Latin American flags. Next to the entrance of the school, a huge poster is found, depicting the Argentinian Marxist guerrilla fighter Che Guevara, who was a central figure in the Cuban Revolution of 1957/58, which hints at a positive attitude towards socialism. Yet, although such symbols link to certain discourses more than to others, it is difficult to evaluate them as necessarily indicating political messages rather than as expressing a general lifestyle in which (formerly¿) non-commercial symbols are 'cool' (for reasons that have to be clarified elsewhere).

The fact that the school has a different commercial strategy from the LA-style school that features in Chapter 5 can be inferred from its advertising material, which is rather amateurish. The flyer mentioned was a black-and-white copy of an invitation to the school and its parties, obviously not created by a professional graphic designer. All other flyers and posters detected during the fieldwork were of the same mediocre quality. Although it may be assumed that this style has been produced on purpose, in order to attract a particular audience, it has to be noted that the school is commercially less successful than the LA-style school, and has fewer students. Nevertheless, it seems that the low quality of the marketing material is also connected to the intentions of the owner of the dance school, which are very distinct from those of the owners of the LA-style school. The latter school spends a lot of money on professional marketing and advertising material, which consequently are of very high quality. On the other hand, it has no rooms of its own and hires the gym of a council community centre to conduct its lessons. The Cuban-style school is situated in a ragged loft, which, despite its relatively bad condition, will be more expensive to rent than a room in a community centre. The priorities differ.

Similar to the LA-style classes, the Cuban-style classes I attended were given by two dance teachers, one male and one female. Both had a Cuban background and a strong Spanish accent in their English. When I attended my first session, the female dance teacher greeted me with kisses on the cheeks and she also said goodbye in the same manner (which is not common with people one does not know according to Australian norms of conduct). The dance sessions were not part of a course but were casual 'drop-in' classes, where one has to pay only if one attends. This option did not exist in the other school. There were only 7–11 other people next to me (it was more than 40 in the LA class). The students' looks and clothing were more similar to my own, although they had a very wide age range (perhaps 20–60 years).

As might be expected from the fact that several teachers in this school have Latin American roots, the ethnic and linguistic composition of the community was significant for understanding the community's ideologies. Although people of many ethnic backgrounds also intermingled in the LA-style community, the value of ethnic 'originality' was constructed differently in the Cuban-style community and, on the part of the 'real' Latin Americans, seemed to be consciously emphasised (for example, in using Latin greeting styles). For dance pupils, contact with 'real' Spanish-speakers was of high value. Most of the pupils were 'white' Australians, usually with a rather high level of education; many were university students. At parties, I also met several European travellers who were staying in Australia on a work and travel visa. Interestingly, the majority of Latin Americans in the school and its parties (who are not teachers) were international students and did not come from Sydney originally but had come to Australia to study. They usually planned to return to Latin America when they would have finished their studies. I met only one Latin American who grew up in Sydney, who, coming from a country where salsa does not belong to the cultural heritage, had not learned salsa from his parents or relatives, but as an adult during a period of political activism in different Latin America countries. Yet, his background as 'Latino' was one of the reasons why he was employed as a dance teacher at the school. The performance of cultural practices and also language use of ethnically 'other' Latin people in this environment played an important role in the school's success, and it is worth mentioning that it was not typically Latin Americans from Sydney who participated. Australian intersections of class and ethnicity probably played a role in not generally making the reproduction of heritage culture attractive for university students (who formed the majority of pupils).

In this community, Cuba is seen as the authentic place of origin of the dance and it is perceived as almost imperative to visit Cuba and to learn to dance from Cubans if one is to become a professional dancer or teacher. Besides the desire to have access to the cultural 'other', this has also to do with the history of Cuba, where a long period of isolation led to an independent development of this particular dance style, so that Cubans are still seen, at least by some, as the only truly legitimate salsa teachers. Dancers and students of Cuban style typically have a relatively intense interest in Latin American culture and are also interested in the Spanish language, and in the case of professional dancers this typically also involves travels to Cuba. Yet, as there are no commercial salsa congresses in Cuba, and as it is usually difficult for Cubans to come to Australia, the transnational connections in the local Cuban-style community of Sydney are much more random and individualised than in the LA-style context, where these are institutionalised in international congresses.

Language in Sydney Cuban Salsa

After I had become anxious that the phenomenon of people being enthusiastic about Spanish might not exist in Australian salsa communities (see Chapter 5), which I first considered to be a methodological problem, I was fascinated to see how the 'same' dance can be appropriated differently in one city, and how this impacts on language ideologies. Overall, Spanish plays an important role in the Cuban-style community, indeed is seemingly omnipresent. The (native English-speaking) owner of the dance school is fluent in Spanish and this ability is very visible in her identity performance, as she speaks Spanish frequently in the school. She communicates in Spanish with her native Spanish-speaking employees but also with those of her students who have learned Spanish. She deliberately employs Latin Americans in order to give access to the 'other' culture and language to her students. The instructions in the salsa lessons are usually in English but the names of moves are kept in Spanish. Not only are many of the school's teachers of Latin American descent, but the receptionist working at the entrance is from Colombia and uses Spanish with anyone who is able to speak it. Indeed, in several interview passages interviewees say that they go to certain places in order to meet native Spanish-speakers and practise Spanish, among them the dance school, where some people go not only to attend a class but also to 'hang out'. The presence of native Spanish-speakers means that Spanish is an often-heard language in the school. Furthermore, the dance school collaborates with a language school that gives discounts to students who learn salsa in the Cuban-style school (see Figure 6.2). Consequently, many dance pupils see it as a goal to acquire a degree of proficiency in Spanish. It must not be forgotten, however, that English remains the dominant medium of communication. As in the LA-style context, flyers and posters are in English and the amount of Spanish words is comparable. It is only single language 'tokens' like *fiesta* or *noche* that are in Spanish.

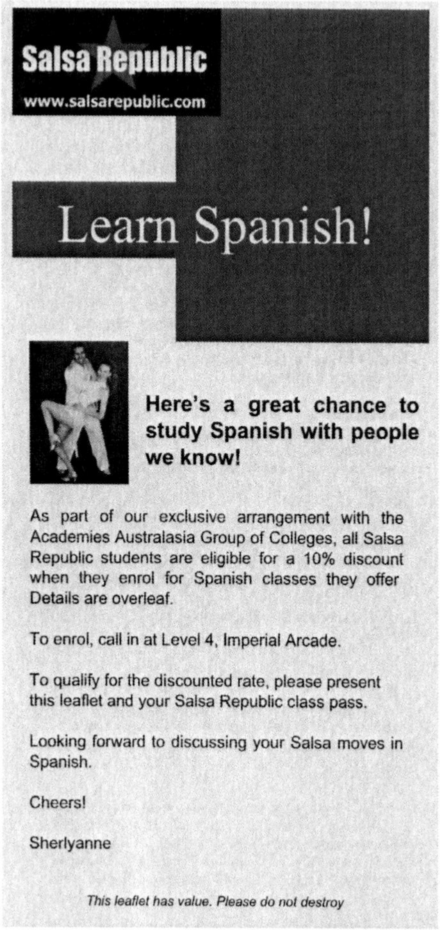

Figure 6.2 Flyer from Salsa Republic promoting language classes, September 2007

Nevertheless, we can maintain that Spanish is much more popular in the Cuban-style community than in the LA-style community.

'Everybody Speaks Spanish Here!'

Similar to the Frankfurt community, the use of Spanish by non-native speakers indicates cosmopolitan awareness, where *cosmopolitanism* means what Hannerz describes, namely, an overall desire to become competent in several semiotic systems, associated with different cultures, and to thus develop a cultural meta-level (see Chapter 2) (this differs from some LA-style interviewees' construction of the term as a kind of global monoculturalism – see Chapter 5). Being able to speak Spanish is prestigious in Sydney Cuban salsa; for instance, the owner of the dance school is very proud of the multilingual environment that is found in her school. When I tell her that, at the beginning of my fieldwork, I had difficulty finding salsa dancers in Sydney who spoke Spanish, the following exchange ensued:

S: Oh God, oh no, éverybody speaks Spanish /here
B: /Oh, real/ly¿
S: /not everybody but (.) almost. (S 5)

It is important for her to emphasise that, in her community, Spanish is an important part of the whole cultural experience. Even though she admits that her first remark may have been a bit exaggerated, she then continues to explain that at least some Spanish is used even by those who do not speak it fluently:

> All the people here,
> that don't speak Spanish in salsa,
> are affected by Spanish and use Spanish words (.)
> all the time (1)
> because it just comes up. (.) in salsa. (S 6)

This perception is obviously very different from the one that is found in the LA-style community, where the acquisition of Spanish is mainly perceived as pointless. In the Cuban-style community, however, speaking Spanish functions as a symbol for in-group membership. Language crossing, the 'use of a language or variety that, in one way or another, feels anomalously "other"' (Rampton, 2000a: 55), which is not part of the ethnic heritage repertoire, has the function of creating a sense of belonging to this particular community, and, as in Rampton's approach, also involves people who are not necessarily fluent in the language. Yet, people who truly belong to the community are usually not monolingual English speakers. As multilingualism is evaluated positively, competence in Spanish – in the following quote also in French – is something that native speakers of English are proud of:

B: And with who do you speak Spanish¿
S: Uhm. Musicians.
Áll the time.

With the musicians.
One of them is Australian even and we always speak in French.
My best friend is from Argentina.
He's my ex.
But he's my best friend now.
We always speak in Spanish.
And uhm (1) musicians, some dancers, some of my instructors,
the girl working at the door is Colombian (1). (S 9)

The dance school owner here lists all the people with whom she speaks Spanish (and French) and thus almost boasts about herself using languages other than English in her everyday life. The emphasis in line 3, 'Áll the time', shows her self-image as someone whose daily life is characterised by multilingual contacts with the 'other'. These contacts imply her ability to speak Spanish, and also her 'artistic' lifestyle, having to do with musicians frequently. Interestingly, although she is asked about Spanish, second on her list is a friend with whom she speaks French, indicating that speaking several languages, especially European languages, is considered in positive terms. The overall approval of multilingual abilities, according to the quote, even leads to English-speakers conversing in French with each other. Being able to use different languages indexes knowledge – 'a little more of the world is somehow under control' (Hannerz, 1996a: 103), and hints at the level of education of the speakers. It thus links to the construction of cosmopolitan identity as discussed in Chapter 2. The symbolic function of multilingualism as indicating cultural and geographical mobility – in other words, the indication of a transnational form of class identity, in which cultural education and travel are vital – is most central in understanding the role of Spanish in the Cuban-style community. I will return to this in the following section.

The evaluation that learning and speaking Spanish is important is shared by all interviewees. The demonstration of multilingual abilities to express cosmopolitan meta-levels is also found in the language use in some of the interview quotes. The school's owner here describes how she uses Spanish with some of her (native English-speaking) pupils:

The other day,
I was speaking to one of them. [in Spanish]
And then the other girl was discovering that.
And came and said
'Oh boy, ¿hablas español¿ Sí, yo tam<u>bién</u>.'
['Oh boy, you speak Spanish¿, Yes, I do too']

> And I'm like
> 'Yóu do tóo¿'
> And we all spoke in Spanish. (S 8)

As can be inferred, non-native Spanish-speakers who are relatively fluent are usually eager to speak Spanish, even if their interlocutor is also an English-speaker. Using Spanish within the interview ('¿hablas español?') makes the narration more authentic; at the same time, it is an opportunity for the informant to present her own language skills in terms of pronunciation to me as her interlocutor, as she is aware that I also speak Spanish. Thus, switching the language in this passage not only has narrative functions but is also an opportunity for the speaker to present herself as knowledgeable and as a connoisseur of Spanish.

In describing the celebration of Spanish in this community, it is of course also interesting to look at the characteristics that are associated with the Spanish language, as 'a definition of language is always, implicitly or explicitly, a definition of human beings in the world' (Williams, 1977: 21 – see Chapter 2). Unsurprisingly, in the interview data, the Spanish language is evaluated extremely positively. It is described as 'cool, social and widely spoken' (JL 11). The language is also considered to be a 'passionate' (G 3–4) language, which links to the heterosexual ideology that is constructed in salsa and related to stereotypical images of the 'Latin lover' (see Chapter 3). Spanish-speakers are described as 'better dancers' (R 18–19), as 'open-minded and fun' (G 6). It is also perceived that native Spanish-speakers 'prefer friendship to money' (G 11). In this last comment, it is apparent that anti-commercial ideologies, as described above, also emerge in language attitudes. Spanish in Cuban-style salsa contexts has connotations of happiness, emotionality, warmth and as 'having soul' (*corazon*, or heart). In this context, the image of Spanish contrasts with the connotations of English, which is in a connotative chain with capitalist development, business and instrumentality (see Chapter 5).

Considering that using Spanish and language crossing to Spanish have a high prestige in the community, it is interesting to note that

> in many cases, crossing is not done in order to pass. Rather, it is done in order to 'index' – point to – certain characteristics which are culturally associated with the group whose behaviour is being appropriated, and which the speaker wants to claim as part of his or her own identity. (Cameron, 2001: 175)

Yet, in interpreting the data from the Cuban-style community (similar to Frankfurt salsa), it is not only the 'characteristics which are culturally associated with the group whose behaviour is being appropriated' that are indexed by using Spanish or Spanish words. It is also the general access to 'others' and, with this, the construction of cosmopolitan identity. Therefore one may interpret the use of Spanish here as a form of 'higher order indexicality' (Silverstein, 2003). While of course the language choice here links to characteristics associated with Latin culture, it has to be taken into account that, at the same time, it is connected to national discourses of educational status, which are interwoven with transnational discourses of mobility. As is true for the LA-style context (see Chapter 5), it is concepts of culture, status and global culture that are co-responsible for the local language ideologies of the community.

Anti-commercialism, Multilingualism and Travel – Creating the Transnational Bourgeoisie

It is enlightening to inspect the language ideologies of the Cuban-style community in relation to national discourses of class belonging and education, and the interconnections of both with transnational discourses on anti-commercialism and traveller culture. Interestingly, the construction of educational status and intellectualism seems to rely partly on a rejection of commercial values. This affects local conditions and I consider this a reason for most Cuban-style dancers' striking dislike of LA-style salsa. The boundary construction of the community towards LA style is a relevant feature in the local community, as being 'non-commercial' and having to do with 'authentic' practices of Latin culture are here markers of difference that create status. A conscious differentiation from LA style can be inferred from the following passage from an interview with a Cuban-style dance teacher:

> Then you have, on the other side (.)
> the other, which is the LA style. (1)
> which I respect (.)
> but I personally don't like.
> I just think that it (.) takes away a lot of the (.) the (.) roots
> and, and the rest of it, where salsa comes from (0.5)
> and tries to make it, um, globalise, ah, it globalises it. (R 9)

As this teacher is aware of the political background of salsa, he criticises what he regards as a cultural disconnection in LA style; later on he describes LA style as 'technical' and 'controlled', terms which for him have negative connotations. Cultural authenticity seems to be important here; the interviewee talks about 'the roots', the cultural and social origins of salsa. It is crucial for the interviewee to consider salsa in its social, political and cultural context, which distinguishes him from those who learn only the dance steps. Dancing Cuban salsa is a practice to express a differentiation from dancers of LA style. It is also interesting to note here that globalisation is obviously regarded as something inherently negative. Taking into account the practices and attitudes that I documented in Chapter 5, one may assume that globalisation here refers to the commercial exploitation of cultural practices.

Negative attitudes to LA style are reflected in discourses on language practices in that 'other' (commercial) salsa style. The owner of the Cuban-style dance school, for example, called salsa dancers and teachers who cannot speak Spanish 'tourists' and said that she found it 'fascinating' that 'people make a living from salsa but never understand the words' (S 11). The fact that LA-style dancers usually do not speak Spanish was seen as a sign of their lack of expertise:

> It is so showy, LA style, it's really funny.
> They don't speak Spanish,
> they only do the silly stuff.
> They haven't been to Cuba. (2)
> Not, nothing against it.
> (laughs)
> But teachers, they all learn Cuban style. (S 22)

There is an evident objection to the practices of the LA-style community and the quote is quite derogatory – 'they only do the silly stuff'. The lack of experience of 'authentic' places of origin of salsa (above all, Cuba) is one reason why LA-style dancers are evaluated as being less sophisticated, next to their lack of Spanish language competence. The informant legitimises her negative comments on the LA community with the phrase 'nothing against it'. The speaker creates a kind of objectivism by saying that she is not generally 'against' LA style. In order to come across as unbiased and objective, she then adds that teachers usually learn Cuban style, not LA style. Those who engage in salsa professionally, according to this informant's view, regard Cuban style as the more interesting ('authentic', 'real') style. Thus, she maintains that the negative evaluation of LA style as being superficial – 'silly' – is not only her own, personal view. Concerning ideologies of language, it is interesting to note that the lack of Spanish is described as evidence of the superficial nature of LA style. Linguistic abilities obviously function as a marker of distinction between the two different salsa communities, and symbolise prestige in demonstrating knowledge. Interestingly, although LA style is of course not a local practice in Sydney, dancers of LA style are here portrayed as 'provincials', as those who do not step out of the common terrain; they are constructed as the 'locals' who have not managed to gain access to cultural systems other than their own (in this respect, LA-style dancers here are like those Hannerz calls *metropolitan locals* – see Chapter 5).

Different attitudes to language and salsa in the two communities reflect in the point of entry to the world of salsa. Some interviewees suggest that Cuban-style dancers often speak Spanish before they start to dance and that this is what differentiates them from LA-style dancers:

G: So, for me, the one thing is,
I didn't come from the dance to the language
but from the language to the dance.
I think this is very different.
B: Yeah, you have a different approach.
G: Yeah, I have a Latin approach,
want to meet people,
not to be on stage or become a champion. (G 1)

According to this speaker, linguistic abilities in Spanish result in a different approach to salsa. She calls this 'a Latin approach', which is based on an interest in socialising with people and not on an interest in competition and performance – she does not want to 'become a champion'. People who first speak Spanish and then learn salsa, in the above construction, want to learn the 'real' Latin salsa, and competence in Spanish makes experience with authentic culture possible. Again, as in the quote above, language ability here clearly serves as a boundary marker to the other local salsa community. Language as a form of boundary marking is not framed conventionally, as it is not ethnic identity that is symbolically represented through language. Rather, multilingualism indexes the ability and the resources to gain the cosmopolitan experience of getting to know other semiotic systems.

Apparently, language choices in this context simultaneously relate to several different orders of indexicality (Blommaert, 2010; Silverstein, 2003). There is, firstly, the local in-group membership of the Cuban-style community, which is distinct from that of the LA-style community; and, secondly, in speaking Spanish, one has access to the transnational 'Latin' community. With regard to the second point, the use of Spanish in Sydney also links to Australian national discourses. For a member of the Australian majority society, being able to speak a second language is a sign of being culturally educated (not 'silly' or 'showy'). As mentioned above, Australia has been reported to have a 'monolingual mindset' (Clyne, 2005; see also Chapter 5) and the number of native speakers of English who have a second language, despite the multilingual composition of the country, is relatively low (Lindsey, 2008). Obviously, speaking a second language as connoting cosmopolitanism links to certain discourses in the national, Australian context, where having learned a second language has a stronger symbolic impact than in contexts where it is normal to do this. Learning and speaking Spanish is not only popular among those who learn salsa but also among other Australians who engage in a 'culturally educated' lifestyle. To have experiences with another culture and to learn another language are a discourse that is meaningful not only in salsa communities; there is, for instance, a Spanish-language 'meet up' group in Sydney, which is the biggest of all 'meet up' groups in Australia (see www.meet-up.com). Although an English-only ideology is largely hegemonic, there are discourses in Australia in which multilingualism is the 'cool factor':

> People are actually waking up to the fact
> that it's actually quite cool to speak a second language.
> Because it's, as Australians,
> we travel a lot to other countries,
> just like the German or Scandinavians.
> So you've got to travel.
> After uni and before you buy a house,
> you have to travel
> and it's very eye opening.
> You understand the value of other cultures, you know,
> it's also the cool factor. (JL 2–3)

Australians are here presented as a nation of travellers and a note is here required on the culture of travelling, which is crucially related to the ideologies of Cuban-style salsa. To travel the world with a backpack, to become a *traveller* or *backpacker*, is a global discourse that produces a particular form of tourism. In this discourse, anti-materialistic values are celebrated (although practices of mass consumption are of course present) and local populations are usually constructed as static and 'different' in order for the backpacker to be able to report on 'authentic' experiences with the 'other' (see Binder, 2005; see also Jaworski & Thurlow, 2004, for a detailed analysis of the interrelations of language, tourism and globalisation). In Australia, the practice of travelling is highly popular and is an almost compulsory component of the socialisation of certain sections and age groups of Australian society. Australian students and young academics, before entering the job market, are eager to travel to other countries, not as 'tourists' but as 'travellers'.

In the quote above, there is a strong class bias, normalised through the construction of the category 'Australian' as people with a university degree who travel around the world and then purchase immovables. This class bias indicates the relevance of Hannerz's concept of cosmopolitanism, which conceives that, for the cosmopolitan, 'the engagement with other cultures is based on the idea of intention, rather than need' (see above and Hannerz, 1996: 105ff.). Travellers go to other places because it is 'cool' and interesting to get to know other cultures, and thus to acquire culturally decontextualised knowledge – meta-cultural knowledge. They then can perform a prestigious identity where they can 'choose to disengage' (Hannerz, 1996a: 104) from their culture of origin (in the case here, this includes the dominant commercial practices of LA style). The ability to have divergent cultural experiences, in the case of Cuban-style salsa with Latin dance, travel and Spanish, thus indicates economic as well as cultural capital (Bourdieu, 1979), and is therefore vital in the construction of class belonging. It is certainly not all Australians who spend their lives in language and dance classes, who enjoy salsa parties, study at a university and buy a house after they have travelled around the world with a backpack. The description of second language acquisition as 'the cool factor' thus can be interpreted as language learning being one aspect of the construction of an Australian social identity that has ties to a transnational upper middle class. Accordingly, in other quotes, Cuban salsa dancers are also described as 'bohemians', who 'are <u>so</u> cultural' and watch SBS[2] (S 10); and, unsurprisingly, those of the interviewees who speak Spanish have all travelled to Latin America or Spain.[3]

The function of multilingualism as an indicator of class also on a national level is supported by the informants' constructions of the language situation in Australia. Despite their emphasis on cultural flexibility, the function of bilingualism and second language learning as indexing belonging to an upper-middle class relies on relatively static conceptualisations of where these 'other' cultures and languages are supposed to be located. Interviewees tacitly reconstruct Australia as a monolingual country, although they generally rejoice in multiculturalism. In the following passage, the speaker, after having spoken about the fact that language learning is more common in Europe, and in discussing why there are fewer language learners in Australia, suggests that the geopolitical situation of Australia makes language learning a difficult enterprise:

It's different in Australia because it's so far.
In Europe you can go for a month to a country.
Or just in your holidays.
And, and you can learn.
You can go over the other weekend to Spain or somewhere. (S 8)

The fact that Australia officially defines itself as being multilingual (Australian Government, Department of Citizenship and Immigration, 2007; Lo Bianco, 2003) seems to go unnoticed by this Australian. Despite everyday contact with people who have native languages other than English (she is the same participant who before emphasised that she uses other languages on an everyday basis), the interviewee explains the low number of Australians who learn other languages with the monolingual and far-off situation of Australia. If, however, language learning requires travel across continents, it becomes a rather privileged activity. To 'really' speak another language necessitates commitment and is described as special and 'life-altering' in the following quote:

Here, it's a major commitment.
So (.) it's usually life-altering.
If somebody here decides to learn another language, it's life altering.
'Cause you need to (.) you know (.) try to somehow to go to that other country. I mean to really speak the language. (S 7)

Regarding the construction of class, it is enlightening that contact with an 'other' is evaluated as 'real' only if it takes place in other countries. Interactions in languages other than English in Australia (although occurring regularly) are not regarded as an experience with 'other' cultures and languages, and it is not conceived that mobility and multilingual language competence can be achieved in Sydney. Nationalist epistemology is effective here and results in Australia being perceived as a monolingual country, despite an opposing actual experience. The dependence of cosmopolitan identity on travel shows that the engagement with different cultures and languages in different countries indexes class identity. It is above all university students who are adherents to this lifestyle, whose flexibility and economic status make it affordable. For engagement with cultural difference to become a symbol of (upper-middle) class belonging, it is necessary that cross-cultural interaction takes place in Havana or Caracas, not in Cabramatta or Fairfield.

To conclude and to return to the research questions, we can state that language ideologies of the Cuban-style community are characterised by highly positive attitudes towards Spanish. The language is associated with positive features and non-native speakers of Spanish are proud of their linguistic abilities. This does not, however, lead to a high presence of Spanish-speakers who permanently live in Australia (which differs from the Frankfurt example). It is mostly 'voluntary bilingualism' (see Ogbu & Simons, 1998), in other words, the bilingual (in some cases symbolic) ability of English-speakers, that is considered an asset. Majority members of Australian society can demonstrate autonomy from their culture of origin and voluntarily engage in an 'other' language, which is indicative of the cosmopolitan functions of this form of multilingualism. Interestingly, this is quite similar for the Latin Americans in the Cuban-style community, who are predominantly international students who do not aim to become Australian. Multilingualism in the Cuban-style community indexes social status, and it is certainly not an accident that it is here mostly Spanish (and not, for example, Filipino or Lebanese) that functions in this sense. Thus, one has to beware of understanding this development of multilingualism becoming 'cool' as being generally empowering for the multilingual populations of Australia. It is above all non-native speakers of Spanish who appropriate an 'other' ('passionate', 'emotional', etc.) world language, as they can afford a lifestyle that includes travel, culture, time and money to spend in dance studios and language classes. Ethnic traits are consumed as 'lifestyle options' (Rampton, 2000b: 10); and despite claims to authenticity, it is not necessarily the native speaker of Spanish who is considered to be on top of the community's social hierarchy. As observed by Rampton, in an age of globalisation, it frequently happens that 'the consumer's personal taste and purchasing power matter as much or more than their early socialization' (Rampton, 2000a: 55).

The discourses to which these language ideologies are tied are mostly discourses on social, economic and cultural status that function across geographical boundaries. As in the previous chapter, several discourses related to different geographical scales come together in the Cuban salsa community in Sydney. Locally developed objection to LA style is linked to anti-commercial attitudes that relate to an appreciation of ethnic 'authenticity' and that indicate a 'culturally' educated background. This is connected to national discourses – being 'culturally aware' and speaking several languages are markers of educational and class difference. The national context here is interwoven with transnational discourses, which positively evaluate contact with the cultural 'other' in order to develop cosmopolitan forms of identity. Geographical and cultural mobility are thus linked to social status and seem to be an element in the construction of transnational cosmopolitan elite identity (this relates to Binder's observation on 'traveller' discourses; see Binder, 2005). Travel across large geographical distances and speaking several languages represent cultural and economic status and these are key aspects in producing social mobility on a national *and* on a transnational scale.

Although traditional power hierarchies seem to be more confirmed than deconstructed, there is a potential for social change, a sign of 'liminality' (see Turner, 1974, quoted in Rampton, 1995a: 233–237), that can be detected in the language ideologies of the Cuban salsa community. Those who cross boundaries and transgress hegemonic everyday reality, paradoxically, are the members of the community who do have an early socialisation with Latin American culture. The boundaries these dancers transgress are not ethnic boundaries but the intersections of ethnicity and class as they have developed in the Australian context of multiculturalism. 'Ethnic' identity in Australia – denoting non-Anglo, non-northern European ethnic identity – instead of being related to a working-class immigrant background (people who need help), can now be linked to cosmopolitanism if the 'other' can speak English. Latin American university students, due to their ability to speak English, can participate in the Cuban-style community. They can perform 'authentic' identity and reappropriate their linguistic and cultural knowledge, as they can also choose to disengage from their culture of origin – they then can also become part of a global '"new class", people with credentials, decontextualised cultural capital' (Hannerz, 1996a: 108). Yet, it is telling that I met only one person who had grown up in Sydney and had started to renegotiate his 'ethnic' identity as 'cosmopolitan'. This differs from the Frankfurt case, where also locally born Spanish-speakers are vitally present. Besides the potential influence of nationalist conservative discourses in the German context, which used to disallow people from gaining German citizenship, and typically brought about strong local reconfigurations of ethnic identity, this may also be an effect of the spatial distribution of the city of Sydney, where 'ethnic' communities do not live in central locations, and thus less easily mix with the more affluent (often 'white') middle classes.

Considering the deconstruction of the concept of language as an entity, the language ideologies of Cuban-style salsa show certain disentanglements of language from ethnic identity. Anglo-Australians here see it as vital to become bilingual speakers of Spanish and English. This form of bilingualism questions national categories, as there is an identification with a language that is not based on ethnic or national belonging. In the construction of boundary marking towards LA style, it is also interesting to observe that bilingualism here expresses local group membership, and not ethnicity.

However, although cosmopolitan multilingual identity does not belong to the traditional national framework of 'one culture – one language', the appropriation of a language in order to participate in an elitist lifestyle does not overcome established intersections of class and ethnicity, and it is furthermore based on the assumption that fixed (national or cultural) categories exist. The reappropriation of the ethnic heritage of native Spanish-speakers as 'cosmopolitan', instead of 'working-class migrant', may be interpreted as the most transgressive act in which a restructuring of established intersections of class and ethnicity can be found. But still, the languages *English* and *Spanish* are considered to be 'given' entities and, in this respect, national frameworks of thought are not questioned.

Concluding, it can be observed that the language ideologies of the Cuban-style community are the result of a combination of discourses – transnational discourses (the development of transnational commercial culture and the construction of cosmopolitan identity), of national discourses (the role of English and the symbolic meaning of bilingualism) and of local discourses (being different from commercialist LA-style dancers). One of the key points in this respect is that languages clearly not only index ethnicity but symbolically function in multiple ways. The theoretical outcomes of these observations are discussed in the final chapter.

Notes

(1) Note that there are of course people in Sydney who dance Cuban-style salsa but who have not learned it in this school and therefore may not belong to the community.

(2) SBS, the Special Broadcasting Service, is a multicultural, multilingual television and radio channel in Australia.

(3) Although Spain is not a country of origin of salsa, it is considered to be an authentic place to dance or learn salsa by some Cuban-style salsa students.

7 Language in a Transnational Age – Mobile Meanings and Multiple Modernities

Big things matter if we want to understand the small things of discourse.
Blommaert (2010: 41)

Transnational social structures have brought about changes that necessitate new approaches to language and, thus, new approaches to the study of language. Categories that have been taken as 'given' – language, the speech community, the native speaker – can no longer be assumed to be unproblematic entities, as they have been co-constructed through discourses that belong to the national era. It was suggested in Chapter 1 that an understanding of how *languages* and their symbolic functions are constituted in discourse is necessary if we are to grasp their role in the creation of community and society in a post-national context. Therefore, the focus of this study is on discourses on language, and interrelated historical, political and social discourses, as they appear in post-national, non-ethnic communities. This is based on an understanding that

> [i]t should be accepted by now that the limitations of a sociolinguistics that focuses exclusively on the details of social interaction should be tempered by the study of structural features that interaction reproduces. It should focus on the link between the characteristics of the linguistic practices and the social and historical conditions of their production, and how they are accepted. This involves how communities constitute objects, how the uses of such objects are contextually determined and how they reflexively interface with other interpretive fields. (Williams, 2010: 18)

The aim of this final chapter is to develop a 'thick description' (Geertz, 1983b; see also Chapter 1) of the constitution of 'objects' that are associated with (transnational) social structures – languages, discourses, cultures, communities – and the underlying structural conditions for their constitution. This leads to questions on more deeply rooted epistemological frameworks, particularly to the concept of *modernity*, and its manifestation in contemporary forms of language and society.

First, I again focus on how local meanings evolve through the interaction of discourses from realms that differ either geographically and in terms of content, which makes visible some more general discursive structures (the non-territorial symbolic functions of language, the impact of discourses of mobility, processes of suppression and elevation of 'truths'). The first section of this chapter relates to the first and second research questions set out in Chapter 1 – which language ideologies are found in salsa communities, and, next to national language discourses, which other societal or cultural discourses co-constitute language ideologies in salsa communities¿ It also looks at some of the structural causes and effects of these discourses. In the second section, the third research question – what happens to the notion of *language* in language discourse in a transnational context¿ – is discussed, together with the related question of how this links to the formation of community in a transnational age. Finally, the discussion of what languages symbolically represent, and the realisation that languages can mean several things at the same time, leads to contemporary academic debates on current developments of modern concepts, among which *language* is one.

Mobile Discourses in Interaction

A key issue in understanding contemporary language ideology is to consider the interaction of diverse discourses in local contexts. Examples from salsa communities in Frankfurt and Sydney show that language ideologies in local contexts are constructed in a knot of different discourses, relating to transnational, national, regional and local spaces so that national discourses are no longer autonomous frames of reference. In this section, I first summarise some important observations from the previous chapters. I discuss the continuing relevance of national discourses in these configurations of interaction, and the non-territorial symbolic functions of languages, among them the ability of languages to symbolise different types of mobility. Thereafter, I introduce some structural effects of the interaction of discourses, namely the fact that transnational processes of fractal recursivity (Irvine & Gal, 2009) emerge, which are linked to the formation of 'blind spots' in discourses.

First, it has become clear that national discourses remain central, but as national frameworks are in interaction with discourses on other scales, national differences 'are no longer taxonomic, they are interactive and refractive' (Appadurai, 1996: 60). Transnational influences have diverse effects on national sociolinguistic economies, depending on their specific shapes. Australia's competitive ideology of belonging, for example, which comes into effect in its regime of citizenship and visa allocation (see e.g. Australian Government, Department of Immigration and Citizenship, 2010), is in a relationship with dominant transnational discourses of neo-liberal capitalism that regards economic profit as the main goal. Due to strong links between these economic discourses and the English language, and due to Australia's colonial history, Australian language discourse constructs an 'English versus other' dichotomy. In Germany, in contrast, more traditional forms of national citizenship ideology interact with transnational economic discourses in diverse ways. This leads to a linguistic hierarchy, with some languages at the top (German, English), some in the middle (Spanish, French) and some (particularly non-European migrant languages) at the bottom.

In the interaction of discourses, we can see that the boundaries constructed by symbolic meanings of languages do not relate only to ethnicity. While national, ethnic or local groups are still important categories, languages also index other, more abstract entities. English in the LA-style salsa community, for example, is tied to transnational competitive discourses, which are part of a capitalist ideology. We find here an evolutionist ideology that considers languages other than English as somehow belonging to the lower ranks of a social order. An important finding in this context is that languages are metaphorically related to imaginations of time, where some languages are regarded as more 'forward' (English) and others as remnants of the past. In the Sydney LA-style community, for example, constructions of time (cultures of migrants are a residue from the past) and of space (these cultures exist in the geographical margins of the city) are constitutive of a social hierarchy. Therefore, symbolic meanings of languages should not be reduced to signifying cultural groups but are complexly interwoven with imaginations of time *and* space and potentially many other cultural concepts. Overall, we see that figures of progress and evolution, which have their origin in modernist discourse (see also below), are crucially related to non-territorial symbolic meanings of languages.

Notions of progress are interlinked with the opposition of *mobility* versus *immobility*. In looking at why some discourses and the accompanying languages become more dominant than others, or why some languages or cultures are seen as more or less static left-overs from the past, the notion of *mobility* comes into play. The so-called *mobility turn* in the social sciences (see e.g. Lenz, 2010: 23ff.; Urry, 2007) considers the social world as non-static, and people, artefacts, material and immaterial resources to be constantly in movement. It attempts to grasp movements between different territorial and non-territorial entities in 'the broader project of establishing a movement-driven social science' (Urry, 2007: 18). While spatial movements of people, symbols and resources first come to mind in this context, a concentration on the interaction of mobile signs and discourses within the same spatial environment is also vital, as mobility is a 'key feature of sign complexes in globalization' (Blommaert, 2003: 611).

Issues of power are crucially interrelated with aspects of mobility. For example, geographical mobility often implies social mobility or expresses the desire for social mobility (as in many migration movements). In the realm of discourse, only linguistic items and discourses that are mobile – that are quoted – gain credibility and power; thus intertextuality and iteration have to be considered as important elements in the reproduction of power structures (see also Pennycook, 2010). Reiteration and mobility are mutually dependent, and tiny fragments of reiterated discourses have been analysed in the previous chapters.[1] Blommaert describes more mobile discourses as more prestigious and suggests that less contextualised discourses are the more mobile ones, also in social terms (Blommaert, 2010: 46). Upward social mobility is, to a certain extent, dependent on the mobility of the linguistic and discursive resources that an individual possesses. In the Cuban salsa communities in Sydney and in Frankfurt, the acquisition of Spanish partly relies on the attempt to take part in 'higher' social and geographical levels or scales. Speaking Spanish here represents a 'scale jump' (Blommaert, 2010: 35) to a higher (decontextualised, 'cosmopolitan') sphere, in which people gain a certain autonomy with regard to their culture of origin and access meta-levels of culture. Yet, in the 'cosmopolitan' Cuban-style salsa communities, engagement with cultural difference becomes a symbol for upper-middle-class belonging only if mobility is indexed in several realms. Cross-cultural interaction and the use of other languages have to take place in Havana, Madrid or San Juan, and not in Preungesheim or Parramatta. Similarly, geographical mobility does not necessarily imply social mobility, as can be inferred from the stigmatisations of illegalised migrants. If linguistic mobility is linked to economic and geographical mobility, however, these links are key aspects of the production of social mobility on a national *and* a transnational scale. A related hypothesis is that we are here observing the development of a transnational class.

English is the prime example of a highly mobile resource that allows access to 'higher' geographical levels. Besides English providing social and geographical mobility, it is a linguistic resource that is mobile itself, as it allows for more intertextual references in more contexts and is thus regarded as more 'central'. English may be in the process of becoming a global 'majority' language, mirroring standardisation processes of national languages (Bourdieu, 1980 [2005]), where non-national languages become 'dialects' and are subordinated in a national hierarchy. Some argue that, on a global level, the relationship between English and other languages 'begins to resemble the conventional relationship between minority languages and the state languages within bilingual states' (Williams, 2010: 60). A comparison with the pre-modern relationship between Latin and 'vulgar' languages may be interesting. Indeed, in some of the observed discourses we find 'new linguistic hierarchies that distinguish between "global/cosmopolitan" and "national/local" languages' (Pujolar, 2007: 83). Nevertheless, it should not be forgotten that English as a global language has not only suppressive functions (for instance allocating 'other' languages to subordinate positions) but also allows for communication among those who are subordinated – English in the LA-style community, for example, is praised for its inclusiveness, which allows for participation regardless of ethnic background.

In Blommaert's framework, 'higher' scales are described as intrinsically less contextualised. Yet, considering the data analysed in previous chapters, it has to be taken into account that the production of 'higher' scales also interacts with local conditions. Speaking Spanish in the Cuban-style community in Sydney refers to a 'higher' (transnational) scale but the particular value of bilingualism is partly derived from the national context of Australia, where relatively low levels of language learning persist. The meaning of global forms as 'less contextualised' is thus linked to the conditions pertaining in particular environments. The production of a relationship to a 'higher' scale through the ability to speak Spanish and English is locally contingent and it is easy to think of other places where bilingualism does not necessarily represent a scale jump. If, therefore, 'higher' scales are defined as 'less contextualised', it has to be considered that the production of 'higher', 'global' or 'transnational' scales is not the production of universally valid and globally functioning spatiotemporal frames. The construction of 'mobility', likewise, does not work in a global and universal context but depends on the discourses that are locally and nationally available. For example, a monolingual repertoire is very rare, if not non-existent, for German university students. Therefore, the value of bilingual abilities with English is not as high a scale jump as the ability to converse in German and English for an Australian university student, for whom fluent bilingualism is a marker of distinction. Nevertheless, some competencies, for example 'native' competence in English, are linked to 'higher' scales in more places than others.

In understanding the construction of power in contexts of mobile resources, it is crucial to see that the local interactions of discourses from several realms can lead to the strengthening of certain meanings as 'true'. The thorny term *fractal recursivity* can be used to describe such processes. Fractal recursivity is 'the projection of an opposition, salient at some level of relationship, onto some other level' (Irvine & Gal, 2009: 403). The notion of *fractal recursivity* refers to the construction of language boundaries in national or ethnic contexts and their effects on internal divisions within these. It is similarly applicable in contexts where transnational discourses are co-constructed through linguistic oppositions. Through processes of transnationalisation, there are wider frames of reference that go beyond national frameworks, and these wider frames have similar effects on the national level as the national level has on its own, inner divisions.

> Center–periphery patterns valid at a worldwide scale also occur for instance within a geopolitical region (think of the expanding EU as a case in point), within one state (the urban versus rural areas) and even within cities, towns or neighborhoods (reflected, often, in real estate prices). (Blommaert *et al.*, 2005: 202)

An example of this is the dichotomy of 'English versus other' languages in the LA-style community, which is mutually reinforced through discourses from the national and transnational scales, and the same type of opposition is found on all three scales. Thus, particularly for members of the LA-style community whose language background is not English, using English represents a kind of double 'scale jump', as English is indexical of 'progress' on the national *and* the transnational level. Considering an example from Sydney's Cuban-style community, the desire to be different from LA style also intersects complexly with discourses from national and transnational scales. Local boundary constructions of Cuban style versus LA style are based on a negative evaluation of transnational commercialist culture, which, in relation to salsa, is criticised as being limited to technique, competition and the accumulation of economic wealth. This is projected onto local levels, where LA-style dancers become indexical of commercially oriented 'tourists' who 'only do the silly stuff'.

On the other hand, the projection of transnational discourses of cultural and linguistic mobility on to local levels allows not only Anglo-Australians to construct local cosmopolitan identities but potentially includes ethnic Latin Americans, who can renegotiate their local minority identity as 'cosmopolitan' also in the Australian, national context. The national order of indexicalities, where 'other' languages signify lower class identity, is reinterpreted through the transnational scale, in which elite multilingualism indexes social mobility and status. Languages other than English gain a place quite high in the local social hierarchy of Cuban-style salsa ('up to date' and in the centre of the city) instead of being located in low socio-economic strata ('in the past' and far out in the west of Sydney). Interestingly, this is slightly different in the German context, where national discourses of ethnic authenticity seem to have a stronger impact, so that Latin Americans are described as proudly forming 'ethnic enclaves'.

In the interaction of discourses from several geographical levels, we can observe not only processes of mutual reinforcement. *Blind spots* can develop, where different types of 'truths' confront each other. 'Blind spots' that occur because of the interaction and simultaneous presence of different discourses in one context require particular attention, as structures of dominance and inequality are easily reproduced through such blind spots (for more examples, see Blommaert, 2010). Blind spots that are based on dominant discourses of transnational distribution can lead to the creation of supposedly 'universal' normativities on a global level. It is typical that 'differences in scales create blind spots or invisible spaces' (Blommaert, 2007: 15). Blind spots are problematic, as they may lead to a misevaluation of the behaviour of the diverse inhabitants of contemporary cities.

> Under conditions of globalization, the increase of sociolinguistic complexity in urban environments due to migration and diaspora can only lead to an increase of such blind spots. The presupposability of linguistic resources, competences, and actual skills is considerably reduced, and more and more people find themselves in spaces where their linguistic baggage has very unclear value. (Blommaert, 2007: 16)

LA-style discourse, for example, constructs a hierarchy between languages and between salsa styles. Colombian-style salsa and languages other than English are primarily related to traditional minority culture, which is regarded as 'undeveloped' and as expressing a 'narrow mind'. Competitive transnational/national ideology results in a 'blind spot' and automatically constructs difference as a difference in value. Here, the normativities of a dominant transnational discourse make it difficult to understand that other discourses have other but equally valid normative structures.

It is important to consider the above insights in current sociolinguistic debates on the role of English worldwide. There is the widespread argument that English serves for international communication, while other languages are local languages, for local identities (e.g. Crystal, 1997; House, 2003; Kirkpatrick, 2007). It is also argued that, therefore, English is no 'threat' to other languages. This usually fails to accommodate the fact that languages can symbolise abstract values that express, for example, 'centrality'. In the case of English, this 'centrality' is based on connotations of economic success, progress or technological advancement. The turn towards English and capitalist-competitive culture is evaluated as cultural 'evolution'. The unproblematised dichotomy of 'English for communication' versus 'other languages for identification' underestimates the power of social discourses that, as in the case of the LA-style community, can result in a tacit stigmatisation of languages other than English. On the other hand, the English language has become an important means of identification in many former colonies, and is not only a tool for communication. To be able to grasp these intricacies, it has been argued that the sociolinguistics of globalisation should be a 'sociolinguistics of mobile resources and not of immobile languages' (Blommaert, 2010: 180). The argument involves the idea that the concept of languages as autonomous structures should be abandoned. This leads to the next section, the discussion of the role of constructions of *language* as an entity in transnational culture.

Truncated Languages and Fragmented Communities

As the role of the nation-state changes due to processes of globalisation, it has been argued that '[c]hanges in the role and nature of the state open up the space for a reconstitutionalisation of the language object' (Williams, 2010: 18). One of the research questions of this study considers the role of the concept of *language* in communities that are not constituted by national belonging. Are languages deconstructed in the discourses of communities that are constituted through salsa dancing? This brings about the related question: if languages continue to symbolise social boundaries, what types of communities do they co-constitute?

First of all, the observed salsa communities show certain forms of disentanglement of the traditional *language–culture* nexus and develop metalinguistic levels. A lot of people identify with languages that do not belong to their cultural heritage. In Frankfurt and in the Sydney Cuban-style community, however, German or Anglo-Australian salsa dancers do not learn Spanish to pass as ethnic 'others' but to index different forms of mobility. Besides class desires that are expressed in these language practices, this overcomes 'common-sense' forms of knowledge, which regard one language as 'normal' or 'natural'. Competence in a non-native language creates a distance from the native language, which implies a certain kind of 'personal autonomy *vis-á-vis* the culture' (Hannerz, 1996a: 104) – and language – of origin. This puts into question a concept of language as a bounded system that describes the world in an all-embracing way. The bilingual or multilingual practices of salsa dancers who engage in cosmopolitan discourses and multi-ethnic communities may thus bring about what has been described as 'dialogic imagination':

> By this I mean the clash of cultures and rationalities within one's own life, the 'internalized other'. The dialogic imagination corresponds to the coexistence of rival ways of life in the individual experience, which makes it a matter of fate to compare, reflect, criticize, understand, combine contradictory certainties. (Beck, 2002: 18)

This is indeed different from language concepts of the national episteme. 'The national perspective is a monologic imagination, which excludes the otherness of the other' (Beck, 2002: 18). National imagination constructs a 'natural' relationship between a language and a *Volk*, which conceives of languages as organs that exist similar to the bloodstream in the body. Through bilingual language practices, a form of language competence may develop beyond the existence of discrete language systems – a meta-language that takes into account the 'coexistence of rival forms of life'.

Yet, in the data introduced, despite potential developments towards dialogic forms of imagination through multilingualism, the national standard languages remain the unmarked 'normal' languages. Yet, it is important to consider that the function and value of different languages in the communities differ to a large extent. The zombie term *language* for the resources associated with 'German', 'Spanish' or 'English', in the local contexts observed, 'obscures the fact that we are facing [...] different, hierarchically ordered resources' (Blommaert *et al.*, 2005: 205). The notion of 'truncated repertoires' (Blommaert, 2010: 103–106) is useful here, as it does not limit language competence to 'complete' knowledge of particular languages. Knowledge of greeting formulae or of emotional expressions is also linguistic knowledge – although this knowledge has been ignored in traditional perspectives on language, where it is the native speaker in a 'homogenous speech community' who is assumed to be the ideal source of information (Chomsky, 1965). People have truncated repertoires of language; not only do they know bits and pieces of many languages but they also have different degrees of knowledge in relation to oral or written, formal or vernacular competence. The notion of 'truncated repertoires' facilitates descriptions of the multilingual abilities of people and at the same time deconstructs the simplified and naturalised concept of 'native' competence as the only 'real' language competence.

Accordingly, the communicative functions of different languages in local communities have to be analysed, not only their mere presence. Although fluency in Spanish is considered an asset in producing an 'up-scaled' and mobile identity in salsa communities, it is obvious that English and Spanish, and German and Spanish, respectively, do not play the same role. It is not necessary to be fluent in Spanish in order to participate in the observed communities. The general medium of communication remains English or German and the use of Spanish is often highly symbolic (for similar observations on multilingualism in the media and in advertising, see e.g. Androutsopoulos, 2007; Piller, 2001a). Spanish is here mostly not a medium of communication. Rather, it is social knowledge of the 'wider social meaning' (Rampton, 1995a: 283) of languages that is indexed through the language practices of salsa communities. Wider social meanings are not only the knowledge of an ethnic other, but the (probably mostly unconscious) knowledge of the ties of different languages to discourses such as class, commercial success, left-wing discourse, being 'up to date', to no longer being the 'frosty middle European', and so on.

Despite the observation that languages are no longer part of a 'monological imagination' and occur in truncated repertoires, it is vital to note that, in the empirical data, the concept of *language* remains a central category. None of the respondents questions the idea of languages as such. Languages clearly serve as boundary markers in social interaction. Thus, multilingual language ideologies as found in salsa communities do not necessarily question standardised varieties of language that are seen as 'belonging' to one culture. Discourses that construct multilingual cosmopolitan identity are related to ensuring

> the privileged position of dominant groups who foster knowledge of powerful 'foreign' languages in their standard forms but delegitimize or ignore other languages and other forms of multilingual competence and performance (e.g. code-switching, heterogeneous skills). (Pujolar, 2007: 78)

In the context of the present study the central languages are three of the most widely spoken, most prestigious languages of the world, while the 'other' languages that informants may use – heritage languages or mixed codes – remain invisible. These types of multilingual ideologies 'can only change very slightly monolingual standardizing ideologies which were hegemonic in modernity' (Heller, 2000: 9). Discourses in which speaking a different language is highly valued differ from monolingual, nationalist orders. However, a critical evaluation of certain truncated multilingual repertoires detects parallels to a general trend in global marketing; this selling of capitalist ideology has been likened to an 'ethnic food court':

> Today the buzzword in global marketing isn't selling America to the world, but bringing a kind of market masala to everyone in the world. In the late nineties, the pitch is less Marlboro Man, more Ricky Martin: a bilingual mix of North and South, some Latin, some R&B, all couched in global party lyrics. This ethnic-food-court approach creates a One World placelessness, a global mall in which corporations are able to sell a single product in numerous countries without triggering the cries of 'Coca-Colonization'. (Klein, 2001, quoted in Piller, 2010b)

Overall, languages, as symbols, continue to be embedded in power hierarchies and clearly mark social boundaries. We are then confronted with the question of what these boundaries relate to. What kinds of 'communities' are we talking about and does it actually make sense to use this term? Clearly, due to the interaction of wider social discourses in local contexts, it is not only the boundaries of local communities of practice that are marked in the examples presented in the earlier chapters. Languages can function as semiotic signs; they can become 'objects of desire, fashion accoutrements and/or marketised life-style options, with "authenticity" becoming as much an issue of commodity branding as a matter of ethnic roots' (Rampton, 2000b: 10). Due to the current dominance of capitalist ideology, relevant factors in getting access to local communities are likely to be shaped by the logics of capitalism – an aspect that is reminiscent of some of the practices in the salsa communities:

> '[L]ife-style' communities […] may be more open and inclusive but […] can also be construed as 'neo-tribes without socialisation' where centres of authority, inner organisation, platforms or statutes are hard to find (Bauman 1992: 25), and where entry is a matter of the consumer's desire, personal taste, shopping skills and purchasing power. (Rampton, 2000b: 16)

The nature of 'community' changes through social processes that transcend the logics of the category of the native speaker, a defining element of traditional speech communities. It is not only important to ask whether speech communities are now local, national or transnational, it is also crucial to question the notion of *community* as such if interaction in a particular language does not necessarily end in the formation of something that speakers perceive as membership of a bounded group. Questioning the concept *speech community* is not new. Linguistic anthropologists and scholars of the ethnography of communication early maintained that '[t]he assumption that speech communities, defined as functionally integrated social systems with shared norms of evaluation, can actually be isolated [has to be] subject to serious question' (Gumperz, 1982: 26). In problematising speech communities, Dell Hymes assumes that shared interactional norms develop on the basis of 'enduring social relationships' (Hymes, 1968: 23) – yet, what if social relationships are not 'enduring'? What if they are fragmented and become more and more individualised?

Salsa communities form a case in point, as these communities are relatively fluid and someone who is an active member this year may be a tango aficionado next year. Salsa communities are different from ethnic groups but they nevertheless generate and in themselves result from social relationships. Social relationships in contemporary communities of practice in leisure and work contexts are different from the traditional relationships of family and community, as they are more fragmented and produce more multiple identities. Even more fragmented are social relationships that develop in virtual social networks such as Facebook, where each member has their own network and individual networks overlap only partly. Milroy's concept of 'dense' and 'multiplex' networks (Milroy, 1987) is here difficult to employ. Individual networks are very complex and depend on individual and diverse factors (interest, time, identity, access to technology, etc.) so that it is difficult to map and compare them in order to study their effects on language. Obviously, interaction that depends on mass media constitutes a separate subject of study but presumably has effects on other types of communication. If contemporary forms of social interaction are taken into account, notions that express 'boundedness' (such as community) become problematic. '[T]he relationships between discourse and community are being dramatically reconfigured in this new age' (Rampton, 2000b: 14). Different conditions of working and living, and different channels of communication lead to different social relationships. What is the relationship between linguistic features and social units, if social units are more temporary, more multiple and spread over larger stretches of space?

As more aspects than national and ethnic descent become relevant in defining status, practices of inclusion and exclusion also function along non-ethnic lines. In the LA-style community, for example, inclusion is mainly based on performance and lifestyle, and thus 'real' Latin Americans – those from the ethnic communities who practise more traditional forms of the dance – are excluded. Exclusion, however, is not based on ethnicity but on discourses of competition and achievement. In contrast to traditional forms of exclusion, rights to access are here not maintained through birth but are tied to economic resources and practices of consumption. Interestingly, some contemporary citizenship regimes have taken up these forms of exclusion and have developed a:

> neo-liberal conception of citizenship that exalts individualism and the spirit of enterprise that enables the citizen to construct her own human capital. It stimulates an assimilationist discourse that distinguishes those who display the dynamism and autodiscipline of the successful native from those who do not display these values, but who resemble the underclass. (Williams, 2010: 225)

At the same time, even countries with neo-liberal citizenship ideologies continue to use national languages as indices of belonging (see e.g. Piller, 2012; Slade & Möllering, 2010). As has been discussed, languages can simultaneously link to ethnic discourses *and* to neo-liberal discourses of economy. Language and community are still tied to each other but in a different and more multiplex fashion; and communities, languages, ethnicities – in other words, modernist categories – still seem to be important analytical concepts in making sense of the world (see also Rampton, 2000b: 16–17).

Multiple Modernities

The concept of *modernity* is complex and has been subject to manifold debates in the social sciences and humanities. It is not the place here to delve into these debates but a very brief definition of the term is required.[2] First, *modernity* is characterised by an opposition to *tradition*, and this distinction involves an evolutionary figure (see also Bauman & Briggs, 2003: 2–12):

> The founding dualism of sociology [whose existence depends on the existence of modern nation-states] is the distinction between traditional and modern society. It has been formulated in numerous ways: as mechanical vs organic solidarity (Durkheim); as status vs contract (Maine); as *Gesellschaft* vs *Gemeinschaft* (Toennies); and as military vs industrial society (Spencer). All of these oppositions have in common that they presume an evolution over time. They are *evolutionary* dualisms. (Beck *et al.*, 2003: 9)

Modernity, in sociological contexts sometimes also called *first modern society* (Beck *et al.*, 2003), is defined by individualisation, sexual division of labour, the nuclear family, closed-off social milieus and particular scientific ideologies (Beck *et al.*, 2003: 4–5). The nation-state, with its internal and external divisions, is characteristic of this type of society. Modernist concepts, among which the nation-state and its accompanying idea of *language* are central, take boundaries of categories to be unambiguous and institutionally guaranteed (Beck *et al.*, 2003: 22). Accordingly, categories of language are understood as having a one-to-one relationship to ethnic/national communities. Yet, as we have seen in Chapters 4–6, this is not the case in language ideologies in salsa communities. Here, as in many other contemporary life-worlds, languages can be indexical of different concepts; these different concepts exist side by side and can also intersect. Some typical relations of languages to other discourses are:

- languages can index culture, ethnicity or nationality;
- languages can index political, social or economic discourses (e.g. English = economic success, Spanish = community values);
- languages can express class status (e.g. as in second language learning to construct cosmopolitan identity);
- languages can be understood as a right (in minority language policy or in education);
- languages can be understood as creating social cohesion (for example in discourses on the integration of migrants);
- languages can be regarded as a product of nature that need to be protected (in discourses on language endangerment).
- languages can be regarded as a resource (e.g. to get a better job).

On a local level, each of these possible functions of languages can serve to mark relationships between different languages and also mark boundaries between social groups that are related to these categories. The picture becomes very complex. Not only do languages represent different types of discourse (e.g. territorial versus economic) but are, furthermore, connected to different types of groups (e.g. local salsa community versus nationality) in different local contexts. As languages are mobile resources and have spread globally, the diversification intensifies. The Spanish language, for example, has very different symbolic meanings in the US (where it is closely aligned with the Hispanic minority) than, for example, in German salsa communities, where it represents access to cosmopolitan 'otherness'.

Additionally, it is not only single languages that can construct multiple boundaries but also notions such as *monolingualism* and *multilingualism*. Multilingualism means different things in different contexts. Knowing Spanish and English is 'elite' in the salsa community in Frankfurt, and means access to economic and cultural capital. Spanish and English language abilities in Sydney can either mean belonging to traditional ethnic communities (heritage multilingualism, language as a right) or can mean elite multilingualism, as in the case of Cuban-style salsa (language to express

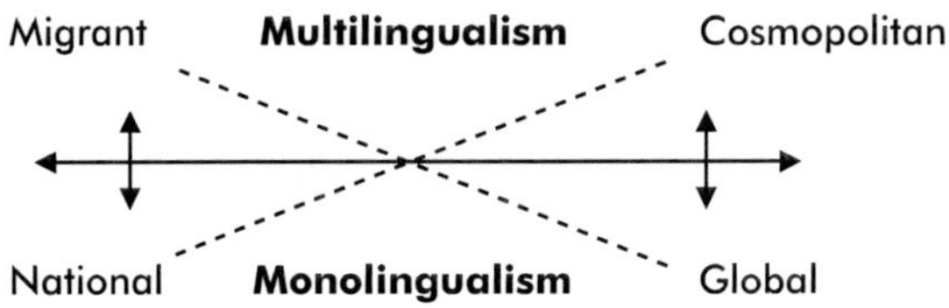

Figure 7.1 The discursive space of the potential meanings of multilingualism and monolingualism in the context of the salsa study

class status). In the observed contexts, the discursive space of the meanings of multilingualism and monolingualism may depicted as in Figure 7.1.

Ideologies that support migrant multilingualism and those that support national monolingualism are clearly opposed and are in conflict with each other. Tendencies of global monolingualism (as in the LA-style community) and ideals of cosmopolitan multilingualism (as in the Cuban-style community) are also two ends of a related scale, where one stands for a globalisation based on universalist values, while the other values a (limited) diversity of languages and cultures. The other relationships are more intricate. National and global monolingualism belong to the same logic in the context where English is spoken and universalist transnational values (e.g. competitive values) are promoted. The LA-style community is an illustrative case. In Germany, however, this relationship is more complicated. While national monolingual discourse that is directed against migrant multilingualism is rather strong, there is a high degree of acceptance of English as a global language in business and academia, and English monolingualism on the global scale is not seen as problematic. Simultaneously, certain types of multilingualism index cosmopolitan elite values. The simultaneous presence of a national monolingual ideology *and* a global monolingual ideology *and* ideologies of cosmopolitan multilingualism can be explained with reference to the multiple boundaries that are constructed through language.

The multiplication of social boundaries drawn by linguistic boundaries confirms the theory of *reflexive modernisation* (Beck *et al.*, 1994, 2003; see also Williams, 2010: 204–205), a sociological theory concerned with the development of modernist categories in contemporary societies. According to this theory, processes of globalisation, liberalisation and technological development have dissolved modern features and boundaries to a certain extent.[3] *Reflexive modernity* (also described as *second modernity*) is characterised by a questioning of modern categories and boundaries, such as nation-states, gender divisions, classes, the subject, rationality, *language*.... It is reflexive in the sense that it problematises its own foundations. Yet, a reflexive questioning of categories as non-'natural' does not necessarily lead to their disappearance:

> So, whereas for many theorists of postmodernism the issue is one of the *de*-structuration of society and the *de*-conceptualization of social science, for re-modernization [reflexive modernization] it is a matter of *re*-structuration and *re*-conceptualization. The goal is to decipher the new rules of the social game as they are coming into existence. The old certainties, distinctions and dichotomies are fading away, but through close investigation of that process we can discover what is taking their place. (Beck *et al.*, 2003: 3)

In approaching society and language as *reflexively modern*, boundaries drawn by modern categories are 'fictive boundaries that are understood as such but [...] are handled as if they were true under the circumstances at hand' (Beck *et al.*, 2003: 20). The recognition of the discursively constructed nature of boundaries is causally related to the fact that, in contemporary transnational contexts, people are confronted with more than one possibility of how to interpret the boundaries drawn by categories. In other words, due to the 'coexistence of rival forms of life' (Beck, 2002: 18), 'the boundaries between social spheres are multiplied' (Beck *et al.*, 2003: 19). Therefore, reflexive modernisation leads to a 'multiplication of the plausible ways in which boundaries can be drawn' (Beck *et al.*, 2003: 19). With regard to *language*, this means that the concept is still relevant but that, as has been shown above, there are different types of discourses to which the category can be 'attached'.

The theory of reflexive modernisation stipulates that both fixed and fluid forms of culture exist side by side. '[I]nstead of an either–or between first and second modernity we face in sociological analysis the challenge of a specific this-as-well-as-that realities: aspects of first and second modernity are interlocked' (Beck *et al.*, 2003: 28), which is indeed what we can find in the discourses on language in salsa communities. 'Modernity has not vanished but it is becoming increasingly problematic' (Beck *et al.*, 2003: 2), and the modernist category *language* remains an analytically relevant concept but loses its status of unproblematised given.

It is enlightening to analyse the different discourses of the different salsa communities with respect to their production of modernist and reflexively modern frameworks. Interestingly, the figure of 'modernity' versus 'tradition', typically distinguishing traditional society from modern society, appears in the discourses of the LA-style community. While LA style and English are conceived as 'modern' (up to date, progress-oriented), Latin American communities and their practices, including their language practices, are regarded as 'traditional'. The evolutionary figure of modernity is clearly reproduced, also with regard to language ideology, and here leads to a monolingual discourse. Yet, it is in a transnational context that the distinctions of the *first modern society* are reproduced. We can observe that transnational discourses bring about not only deconstruction but may even impose 'traditional' modernist models of culture and society. The status of English as a global lingua franca frequently reproduces the division between tradition (other languages) and modernity (English). English is related to a 'universalist' type of cosmopolitanism that constructs an evolutionist image of the world, embedded in neo-liberal capitalist regimes.

The different conceptualisations of cosmopolitanism that have been documented in the empirical data of this study can also be interpreted as linking to either *first* or to *second modernity*. The LA-style community constructs a monolingual, monocultural, modernist figure of 'cosmopolitanism'. Some social scientists see an overall 'new emphasis on universalism' in transnational discourses (Habermas, 1996, quoted in Williams, 2010: 221) and assume a 'real danger of a link between economic hegemony, global law and the imposition of "universal values"' (Williams, 2010: 221). In the LA-style community, indeed, economic hegemony – competitive ideology – is constructed as a 'universal' value. The Cuban-style community, on the other hand, accepts and rejoices in diversity and shows tendencies of 'dialogic imagination' and an understanding of categories as non-natural. The notion of 'cosmopolitanism' here links more closely to Hannerz's definition, which embraces the development of meta-cultural awareness – the reflexively modern recognition that there are different and multiple ways of constructing boundaries. However, this discourse has its own pitfalls. Not *all* languages have the same status and the notion of the 'market masala' characterises the type of commodification that takes place in these contexts.

Considering these intricacies of transnational discourses on language and culture, we can confirm that '[t]he old certainties, distinctions and dichotomies are fading away' and that it should be 'through close investigation of that process [that] we can discover what is taking their place' (Beck *et al.*, 2003: 3). This puts into question modernist approaches to the study of language. The modernist 'linguist's choice [is] often to imagine separate speech communities with their own boundaries, sovereignty, fraternity and authenticity' (Pratt, 1987: 56). This choice belongs, in the terminology of reflexive modernisation, to first modernity, as the category of speech community is taken as given and forms the basis for subsequent study. The discursive space in which languages find themselves has become multiple and this necessitates what Beck calls 'methodological cosmopolitanism', a methodology that 'rejects the either–or principle and assembles the this-as-well-as-that principle' (Beck, 2002: 19). Although languages remain analytically relevant, linguists have to be aware that *languages* are culturally constructed categories that have multiple social functions in multiple social spaces. Languages and accompanying notions, such as *grammaticality* or the *native speaker*, are culturally contingent categories. This has to be taken into account in order to avoid analytical imprecision.

Summarising the above analysis, it has been demonstrated that the idea of *language* remains a vital concept. Standardised varieties of language are still highly salient in constructing social boundaries. The 'zombie' *nation* is still alive: national language ideologies, national regimes of 'integration', their interaction with global, regional and local discourses, and their consequences for those who are confronted with them continue to impact on other discourses. National standard languages play an important role in creating elite identity, including in transnational realms; however, contemporary elite identity is characterised by different types of mobility (social, geographical, linguistic, etc.) that express ties to transnational scales. Through the links to transnational realms, the ties of languages to discourses that do not constitute groups (but, say, as explicated above, relate to 'progress') become more visible. It is thus possible to speak about *languages* without giving them a 'natural' status but one may propose that there are different discursive processes that lead to certain 'truths' becoming more dominant than others.

Another effect of transnationalism is that language groups have become de-essentialised, as membership of language groups is often no longer understood as a quasi-natural process. Access to cultural groups is not always dependent on heritage but various options have become possible. A capitalist ideology of performance and success here often interacts with other features in constructing belonging. And yet, although links between languages and groups are no longer exclusive sources in defining symbolic meanings of languages, such links have not ceased to exist. The question of how 'linguistic units come to be linked with social units' (Gal & Irvine, 1995: 970) in transnational cultures can thus be answered tentatively by saying that the links between social units and linguistic units have diversified. *Iconisation*, the process by which a language becomes an index for a group (see Irvine & Gal, 2000), is still an important factor in understanding the fields of social knowledge that are co-responsible for the discursive construction of linguistic units. Yet, the crucial observation in this context is that languages do not only index groups or group belonging. They are more diversified and more complex and less easy to define. Studies on the link between languages and communities will still be of vital interest in future research on the sociolinguistics of globalisation.

Coming to a final conclusion, the above analyses may have inspired some thought about which 'resources [we] must have in order to transform the exclusive nation-state organized societies into inclusive cosmopolitical societies and states' (Beck *et al.*, 2003: 8). A multilingual 'cosmopolitan' perspective, that encompasses the aim of learning 'other' semiotic systems, despite consumerist pitfalls and class connotations, may be constructive in overcoming social evolutionism and monolingual, monocultural universalism. The ability to regard the language and culture of heritage as relative and contingent, and not as 'normal' or 'natural', is an important aspect of such a cosmopolitan vision of the world, which may 'lead to the compassion and humanization of others' (Gilroy, 2005: 67).

Notes

(1) The general power of iterability is subject of theoretical discussions elsewhere (e.g. Butler, 2003; Pennycook, 2010; Wirth, 2002).

(2) I base this definition on the discussion by Beck *et al.* (2003) but it has to be noted that there are many different conceptualisations. For closer insights into how modernity impacts on the epistemology of linguistics, see Bauman and Briggs (2003).

(3) It has to be noted that the theory of reflexive modernity has Eurocentric tendencies, as it 'takes for granted that the institutions that second modernity dissolves [e.g. the nation-state, the welfare state, or gainful employment societies] are there in the first place' (Beck *et al.*, 2003: 7).

References

Alén, O. (1984) *De Lo Afrocubano a La Salsa: Géneros Musicales De Cuba*. San Juan: Cubanacán.

Alter, S. (1999) *Darwin and the Linguistic Image: Language, Race and Natural Theology in the Nineteenth Century*. Baltimore, MD: John Hopkins University Press.

Anderson, B. (1985) *Imagined Communities*. London: Verso.

Androutsopoulos, J. (2007) Bilingualism in the mass media and on the internet. In M. Heller (ed.) *Bilingualism: A Social Approach* (pp. 207–230). Basingstoke: Palgrave Macmillan.

Anzaldúa, G. (1987) *Borderlands/ La Frontera: The New Mestiza*. San Francisco, CA: Aunt Lute Books.

Aparicio, F.R. (1998) *Listening to Salsa: Gender, Latin Popular Music, and Puerto Rican Cultures*. Hanover, NH: Wesleyan University Press.

Aparicio, F.R. (2002) La Lupe, La India, and Celia: Towards a feminist genealogy of salsa music. In L. Waxer (ed.) *Situating Salsa: Global Markets and Local Meanings in Latin Popular Music* (pp. 135–160). New York: Routledge.

Aparicio, F.R. and Jáquez, C. (eds) (2003) *Musical Migrations: Transnationalism and Cultural Hybridity in Latin/o America*. Basingstoke: Palgrave Macmillan.

Appadurai, A. (1996) *Modernity at Large: Cultural Dimensions of Globalization*. Minneapolis, MN: University of Minnesota Press.

Appadurai, A. (1998) Globale ethnische Räume: Bemerkungen und Fragen zur Entwicklung einer transnationalen Anthropologie. In U. Beck (ed.) *Perspektiven der Weltgesellschaft* (pp. 11–40). Frankfurt am Main: Suhrkamp.

Arens, H. (1969) *Sprachwissenschaft. Der Gang ihrer Entwicklung von der Antike bis zur Gegenwart. Band 1. Von der Antike bis zum Ausgang des 19. Jahrhunderts*. Frankfurt am Main: Athenäum Fischer Taschenbuchverlag.

Arnaut, K. (2012) Super-diversity: Elements of an emerging perspective. *Diversities* 14, 1–16.

Auer, P. (1999) From codeswitching via language mixing to fused lects: Toward a dynamic typology of bilingual speech. *International Journal of Bilingualism* 3, 309–332.

Auer, P. (2007) Introduction. In P. Auer (ed.) *Style and Social Identities: Alternative Approaches to Linguistic Heterogeneity* (pp. 1–21). Berlin: de Gruyter.

Australian Bureau of Statistics (2007) *Migration: Permanent Additions to Australia's Population*. Available at http://www.abs.gov.au/AUSSTATS/abs@.nsf/7d12b0f6763c78caca257061001cc588/928af7a0cb6f969fca25732c00207852!OpenDocument (accessed 19 February 2014).

Australian Citizenship Test Review Committee (2008) *Moving Forward ... Improving Pathways to Citizenship. A Report by the Australian Citizenship Test Review Committee.* Barton, ACT: Commonwealth of Australia.

Australian Government (2009) The policy context (ch. 1). In *Report of the Review of Settlement Services for Migrants and Humanitarian Entrants*. Available at www.immi.gov.au/media/publications/settle/_pdf/chap01web.pdf (accessed 20 February 2014).

Australian Government, Department of Citizenship and Immigration (2007) *Accessible Government Services For All*. Available at www.immi.gov.au/about/reports/accessible_government/accessible_government_2006/_pdf/accessible_government_part1.pdf (accessed 20 February 2014).

Australian Government, Department of Immigration and Citizenship (2009) *Adult Migrant English Program (AMEP)*. Available at www.immi.gov.au/living-in-australia/help-with-english/amep (accessed 10 March 2014).

Australian Government, Department of Immigration and Citizenship (2010) *Fact Sheet 20 – Migration Program Planning Levels*. Available at www.immi.gov.au/media/fact-sheets/20planning.htm (accessed 20 February 2014).

Bakhtin, M.M. (1935 [2006]) The problem of speech genres. In A. Jaworski and N. Coupland (eds) *The Discourse Reader* (pp. 98–107). London: Routledge.

Barbour, S. and Carmichael, C. (2000) *Language and Nationalism in Europe*. Oxford: Oxford University Press.

Bauman, R. and Briggs, C.L. (2003) *Voices of Modernity: Language Ideologies and the Politics of Inequality*. Cambridge: Cambridge University Press.

Bauman, Z. (1992) Survival as a social construct. In M. Featherstone (ed.) *Cultural Theory and Cultural Change* (pp. 1–36). London: Sage.

Bauman, Z. (1999) *Culture as Praxis.* London: Sage.

Beck, U. (1997) *Was ist Globalisierung?* Frankfurt am Main: Suhrkamp.

Beck, U. (2001) Zombie categories: Interview with Ulrich Beck. In U. Beck and E. Beck-Gernsheim (eds) *Individualization: Institutionalised Individualism and Its Social and Political Consequences* (pp. 202–212). London: Sage.

Beck, U. (2002) The cosmopolitan society and its enemies. *Theory, Culture and Society* 19, 17–44.

Beck, U., Bonss, W. and Lau, C. (2003) The theory of reflexive modernization: Problematic hypotheses and research programme. *Theory, Culture and Society* 20, 1–33.

Beck, U., Giddens, A. and Lash, S. (1994) *Reflexive Modernization: Politics, Tradition and Aesthetics in the Modern Social Order*. Cambridge: Polity Press.

Behrens, R. (2003) *Postmoderne*. Hamburg: EVA.

Berger, P.L. and Luckmann, T. (1966) *The Social Construction of Reality*. Garden City, NY: Doubleday.

Berríos-Miranda, M. (2002) Is salsa a musical genre? In L. Waxer (ed.) *Situating Salsa: Global Markets and Local Meanings in Latin Popular Music* (pp. 23–50). New York: Routledge.

Bhabha, H.K. (1994) *The Location of Culture*. London: Routledge.

Billig, M. (1995) *Banal Nationalism*. London: Sage.

Binder, J. (2005) *Globality: Eine Ethnographie über Backpacker*. Münster: Lit Verlag.

Bishop, P. (1989) *The Myth of Shangri-La: Tibet, Travel Writing, and the Western Creation of Sacred Landscape.* Berkeley, CA: University of California Press.

Block, D., Gray, J. and Holborow, M. (2012) *Neoliberalism and Applied Linguistics*. London: Routledge.

Blommaert, J. (1999) *Language Ideological Debates*. Berlin: de Gruyter.

Blommaert, J. (2003) Commentary: A sociolinguistics of globalization. *Journal of Sociolinguistics* 7, 607–623.

Blommaert, J. (2005) *Discourse*. Cambridge: Cambridge University Press.

Blommaert, J. (2007) Sociolinguistic scales. *Intercultural Pragmatics* 4, 1–19.

Blommaert, J. (2010) *The Sociolinguistics of Globalization*. Cambridge: Cambridge University Press.

Blommaert, J. and Rampton, B. (2011) Language and superdiversity. *Diversities* 13, 1–21.

Blommaert, J. and Verschueren, J. (1998) The role of language in European nationalist ideologies. In B.B. Schieffelin, K.A. Woolard and P.V. Kroskrity (eds) *Language Ideologies: Practice and Theory* (pp. 189–210). Oxford: Oxford University Press.

Blommaert, J., Collins, J. and Slembrouck, S. (2005) Spaces of multilingualism. *Language and Communication* 25, 197–216.

Bourdieu, P. (1979) *Die feinen Unterschiede. Kritik der gesellschaftlichen Urteilskraft*. Frankfurt am Main: Suhrkamp.

Bourdieu, P. (1980 [2000]) The production and reproduction of legitimate language. In L. Burke *et al.* (eds) *The Routledge Language and Cultural Theory Reader* (pp. 467–477). London: Routledge.

Bourdieu, P. (1980 [2005]) *Was heisst Sprechen? Die Ökonomie des Sprachlichen Tausches*. Vienna: Braumüller.

Bublitz, H. (2003) *Diskurs*. Bielefeld: Transcript Verlag.

Bullock, A. (1975) *Bullock Report: A Language for Life*. London: HMSO.

Burawoy, M. (1998) The extended case method. *Sociological Theory* 16, 4–33.

Buschkowsky, H. (2012) *Neukölln ist Überall*. Berlin: Ullstein.

Butler, J. (2003) Identity, deconstruction and politics. In M. Gergen and K.J. Gergen (eds) *Social Construction: A Reader* (pp. 129–131). London: Sage.

Cameron, D. (1995) *Verbal Hygiene*. London: Routledge.

Cameron, D. (2001) *Working with Spoken Discourse*. London: Sage.

Carnie, A. (2013) *Syntax: A Generative Introduction*. Oxford: Wiley-Blackwell.

Castells, M. (2002) *Die Macht der Identität. Teil 2 der Trilogie 'Das Informationszeitalter'*. Opladen: Leske & Budrich.

Chomsky, N. (1965) *Aspects of the Theory of Syntax*. Cambridge, MA: MIT Press.

Clifford, J. (1994) Diasporas. *Cultural Anthropology* 9, 302–338.

Clyne, M. (2005) *Australia's Language Potential*. Sydney: UNSW Press.

Collins, J. and Slembrouck, S. (2008) *Is Class Relevant in Constructing a Multilingual Europe?* Working Papers in Urban Language and Literacies 52, King's College London. Available at www.kcl.ac.uk/sspp/departments/education/research/ldc/publications/workingpapers/download.aspx (accessed 20 February 2014).

Commission of the European Communities (2005) *A New Framework Strategy for Multilingualism*. Brussels: Communication from the Commission to the Council, the European Parliament, the European Economic and Social Committee of the Regions. Available at http://eur-lex.europa.eu/LexUriServ/LexUriServ.do?uri=COM:2005:0596:FIN:EN:PDF (accessed 20 February 2014).

Coupland, N. and Jaworski, A. (2004) Sociolinguistic perspectives on metalanguage: Reflexivity, evaluation and ideology. In A. Jaworski, N. Coupland and D. Galasinski (eds) *Metalanguage: Social and Ideological Perspectives* (pp. 15–51). Berlin: de Gruyter.

Creese, A. (2008) Linguistic ethnography. In N. Hornberger (ed.) *Encyclopedia of Language and Education* (pp. 229–241). New York: Springer.

Crystal, D. (1997) *English as a Global Language*. Cambridge: Cambridge University Press.

Djité, P. (2006) Shifts in linguistic identities in a global world. *Language Problems and Language Planning* 30, 1–20.

Doleschal, U. (2002) *Das generische Maskulinum im Deutschen. Ein historischer Spaziergang durch die deutsche Grammatikschreibung von der Renaissance bis zur Postmoderne*. Available at www.linguistik-online.de/11_02/doleschal.pdf (accessed 20 February 2014).

Errington, J. (2008) *Linguistics in a Colonial World: A Story of Language, Meaning and Power*. Malden, MA: Blackwell.

Farley, C.J. (1999) Latin music pops. *Time*, 24 May, pp. 40–45.

Farrell, E. (2008) Negotiating identity: Discourses of migration and belonging. Unpublished PhD thesis, Macquarie University.

Foucault, M. (1970) *The Order of Things*. New York: Vintage Books.

Foucault, M. (1970 [2000]) The discourse of language. In L. Burke, T. Crowley and A. Girvin (eds) *The Routledge Language and Cultural Theory Reader* (pp. 231–240). London: Routledge.

Foucault, M. (1972) *The Archaeology of Knowledge*. London: Tavistock.

Foucault, M. (1972 [2001]) *Die Ordnung des Diskurses*. Frankfurt am Main: Fischer Verlag.

Foucault, M. (1973) *Archäologie des Wissens*. Frankfurt am Main: Suhrkamp.

Foucault, M. (1979) *The History of Sexuality. Vol. 1: An Introduction*. London: Allen Lane.

Foucault, M. (1980a) *Power/Knowledge: Selected Interviews and Other Writings 1972–1977*. New York: Pantheon Books.

Foucault, M. (1980b) Truth and power. In G. Colin (ed.) *Power/Knowledge: Selected Interviews and Other Writings 1972–1977* (pp. 109–133). New York: Harvester Wheatsheaf.

Gal, S. and Irvine, J.T. (1995) The boundaries of languages and disciplines: How ideologies construct difference. *Social Research* 62, 967–1001.

Gal, S. and Woolard, K.A. (1995) Special issue: Constructing languages and publics. *Pragmatics* 5, 129–280.

Gee, J.P. (2005) *An Introduction to Discourse Analysis*. London: Routledge.

Geertz, C. (1973) *The Interpretation of Cultures*. New York: Basic Books.

Geertz, C. (ed.) (1983a) *Dichte Beschreibung: Beiträge zum Verstehen kultureller Systeme*. Frankfurt am Main: Suhrkamp.

Geertz, C. (1983b) Dichte Beschreibung: Bemerkungen zu einer deutenden Theorie von Kultur. In C. Geertz (ed.) *Dichte Beschreibung: Beiträge zum Verstehen kultureller Systeme* (pp. 7–43). Frankfurt am Main: Suhrkamp.

Geller, A. (2005) *Diskurs von Gewicht*. Köln: Pappy Rossa.

Giddens, A. (1990) *The Consequences of Modernity*. Stanford, CA: Stanford University Press.

Gilroy, P. (1987) *There Ain't No Black in the Union Jack*. London: Hutchison.

Gilroy, P. (2005) *After Empire: Multiculture or Postcolonial Melancholia*. New York: Columbia University Press.

Glick Schiller, N., Basch, L. and Blanc, C.S. (1997) From immigrant to transmigrant: Theorizing transnational migration. In L. Pries (ed.) *Transnationale Migration* (pp. 121–140). Baden Baden: Nomos.

Gobo, G. (2008) *Doing Ethnography*. London: Sage.

Gogolin, I. (1994) *Der monolinguale Habitus der multilingualen Schule*. Münster: Waxmann.

Gogolin, I. (2001) Sprachenvielfalt durch Zuwanderung – Ein verschenkter Reichtum in der Arbeitswelt. Paper presented at the Good Practice Centre Workshop, Förderung von MigrantInnen in der beruflichen Bildung durch sprachbezogene Angebote, Bonn. Available at http://www.good-practice.de/18_gesamt_Doku.pdf (accessed 20 February 2014).

Gogolin, I. and Reich, H. (2001) Immigrant languages in Federal Germany. In G. Extra and D. Gorter (eds) *The Other Languages of Europe* (pp. 193–214). Clevedon: Multilingual Matters.

Gogolin, I., Neumann, U. and Reuter, L. (eds) (2001) *Schulbildung Für Kinder aus Minderheiten in Deutschland 1989–1999*. Münster: Waxmann.

Gruner, S. (2010) 'The others don't want…'. Small-scale segregation: Hegemonic public discourses and racial boundaries in German neighbourhoods. *Journal of Ethnic and Migration Studies* 36, 275–292.

Gumperz, J.J. (1982) *Discourse Strategies*. Cambridge: Cambridge University Press.

Gumperz, J.J. and Hymes, D. (1964) Preface to 'Special issue: The ethnography of communication'. *American Anthropologist* 66, v.

Habermas, J. (1996) *La Paix Perpetuelle, Le Bicentenaire D'une Idee Kantienne*. Paris: CERF.

Hall, S. (1992) Race, culture, and communications: Looking backward and forward at cultural studies. *Rethinking Marxism* 5, 10–18.

Hall, S. (1994) Kulturelle Identität und Diaspora. In S. Hall *Rassismus und kulturelle Identität* (pp. 26–43). Hamburg: Argument Verlag.

Halm, D. and Sauer, M. (2006) Parallelgesellschaft und ethnische Schichtung. *Aus Politik und Zeitgeschichte* 1–2, 18–24.

Hamel, R.E. (1997) Language conflict and language shift: A sociolinguistic framework for linguistic human rights. *International Journal of the Sociology of Language* 127, 105–134.

Hannerz, U. (1996a) Cosmopolitans and locals in world culture. In U. Hannerz *Transnational Connections: Culture, People, Places* (pp. 102–111). London: Routledge.

Hannerz, U. (1996b) *Transnational Connections: Culture, People, Places*. London: Routledge.

Hartmann, J. and Klesse, C. (2007) Heteronormativität. Empirische Studien zu Geschlecht, Sexualität und Macht – Eine Einführung. In J. Hartmann, C. Klesse, P. Wagenknecht, B. Fritzsche and K. Hackmann (eds) *Heteronormativität. Empirische Studien zu Geschlecht, Sexualität und Macht* (pp. 1–15). Wiesbaden: VS Verlag für Sozialwissenschaften.

Heath, S.B. (1989) Language ideology. In E. Barnouw (ed.) *International Encyclopedia of Communications* (pp. 393–395). Oxford: Oxford University Press.

Heller, M. (2000) Bilingualism and identity in the post-modern world. *Estudios de Sociolingüistica* 1, 9–24.

Heller, M. (2007a) Bilingualism as ideology and practice. In M. Heller (ed.) *Bilingualism: A Social Approach* (pp. 1–22). Basingstoke: Palgrave Macmillan.

Heller, M. (2007b) The future of 'bilingualism'. In M. Heller (ed.) *Bilingualism: A Social Approach* (pp. 340–345). Basingstoke: Macmillan.

Heller, M. and Duchêne, A. (eds) (2012) *Language and Late Capitalism: Pride and Profit*. New York: Routledge.

Hellinger, M. (2000) Feministische Sprachpolitik und politische Korrektheit – Der Diskurs der Verzerrung. In K. Eichhoff-Cyrus and R. Hoberg (eds) *Die Deutsche Sprache zur Jahrtausendwende: Sprachkultur oder Sprachverfall¿* (pp. 177–191). Mannheim: Duden Verlag.

Hoffmann, C. (1991) *An Introduction to Bilingualism*. London: Longman.

Holmes, J. (2008) *An Introduction to Sociolinguistics*. London: Longman.

Holmes, J. and Meyerhoff, M. (1999) The community of practice: Theories and methodologies in language and gender research. *Language in Society* 28, 173–183.

Hopper, P. (1988) Emergent grammar and the a priori grammar postulate. In D. Tannen (ed.) *Linguistics in Context: Connecting Observation and Understanding* (pp. 117–134). Norwood, NJ: Ablex Publishers.

Hornberger, N.H. (2005) Introduction. Heritage/community language education: US and Australian perspectives. *International Journal of Bilingual Education and Bilingualism* 8, 101–108.

Hosokawa, S. (2002) Salsa no tiene fronteras: Orquesta De La Luz and the globalization of popular music. In L. Waxer (ed.) *Situating Salsa: Global Markets and Local Meanings in Latin Popular Music* (pp. 289–312). New York: Routledge.

House, J. (2003) English as a lingua franca: A threat to multilingualism? *Journal of Sociolinguistics* 7, 556–578.

Hymes, D. (1968) Linguistic problems in defining the concept of 'tribe'. In J. Helm (ed.) *Essays on the Problem of the Tribe: Proceedings of the 1967 Annual Spring Meeting of the American Ethnological Society* (pp. 23–48). Washington, DC: University of Washington Press.

Irvine, J.T. (1989) When talk isn't cheap: Language and political economy. *American Ethnologist* 16, 248–267.

Irvine, J.T. (1995) The family romance of colonial linguistics: Gender and family in nineteenth-century representations of African languages. *Pragmatics* 5, 139–153.

Irvine, J.T. (2001) 'Style' as distinctiveness: The culture and ideology of linguistic differentiation. In P. Eckert and J.R. Rickford (eds) *Style and Sociolinguistic Variation* (pp. 21–43). Cambridge: Cambridge University Press.

Irvine, J.T. and Gal, S. (2000) Language ideology and linguistic differentiation. In P.V. Kroskrity (eds) *Regimes of Language: Ideologies, Polities and Identities* (pp. 35–83). Santa Fe, NM: School of American Research Press.

Irvine, J.T. and Gal, S. (2009) Language ideology and linguistic differentiation. In A. Duranti (eds) *Linguistic Anthropology: A Reader* (pp. 402–434). Oxford: Wiley Blackwell.

Jaworski, A. and Coupland, N. (2006) Introduction: Perspectives on discourse analysis. In A. Jaworski and N. Coupland (eds) *The Discourse Reader* (pp. 1–37). London: Routledge.

Jaworski, A. and Thurlow, C. (2004) Language, tourism and globalization: Mapping new international identities. In S.H. Ng, C.N. Candlin and C.Y. Chiu (eds) *Language Matters: Communication, Identity, and Culture* (pp. 297–321). Hong Kong: City University of Hong Kong Press.

Jayasuriya, L., Walker, D. and Gothard, J. (eds) (2003) *Legacies of White Australia: Race, Culture and Nation*. Crawley: University of Western Australia Press.

Johnstone, B. (2008) *Discourse Analysis*. Oxford: Blackwell.

Joseph, J.E. and Taylor, T.J. (eds) (1990) *Ideologies of Language*. London: Routledge.

Jupp, J. (2001) *The Australian People: An Encyclopedia of the Nation, Its People and Their Origins*. Cambridge: Cambridge University Press.

Kearney, R. (1988) *The Wake of Imagination*. Minneapolis, MN: University of Minnesota Press.

Kipp, S., Clyne, M. and Pauwels, A. (1995) *Immigration and Australia's Language Resources*. Canberra: Australian Government Publishing Service.

Kirkpatrick, A. (2007) Linguistic imperialism? English as a global language. In M. Hellinger and A. Pauwels (eds) *Handbook of Language and Communication: Diversity and Change (Handbooks of Applied Linguistics [HaL])* (pp. 333–364). Berlin: de Gruyter.

Klein, N. (2001) *No Logo: Taking Aim at the Brand Bullies*. New York: Picador.

Kohut, K. (1996) *Deutsche in Lateinamerika – Lateinamerika in Deutschland*. Frankfurt am Main: Vervuert.

Koopmans, R. (2001) Deutschland und seine Einwanderer: Ein gespaltenes Verhältnis. *Blätter für deutsche und internationale Politik* 2, 1–28.

Kress, G. and van Leeuwen, T. (2001) *Multimodal Discourse: The Modes and Media of Contemporary Communication*. London: Hodder Arnold.

Kroskrity, P.V. (2000a) Regimenting languages: Language ideological perspectives. In P.V.

Kroskrity (ed.) *Regimes of Language: Ideologies, Polities, and Identities* (pp. 1–34). Santa Fe, NM: School of American Research Press.

Kroskrity, P.V. (ed.) (2000b) *Regimes of Language: Ideologies, Polities and Identities*. Santa Fe, NM: School of American Research Press.

Kroskrity, P.V. (2001) Language ideology. In J.-O. Östman and J. Verschueren (eds) *Handbook of Pragmatics* (pp. 1–24). Amsterdam: Benjamins. Available at https://benjamins.com/online/hop (accessed 20 February 2014).

Lacoste, V. and Mair, C. (2012) Authenticity in creole-speaking contexts: An introduction. *Zeitschrift für Anglistik und Amerikanistik* 60, 211–215.

Lave, J. and Wenger, E. (1991) *Situated Learning: Legitimate Peripheral Participation*. Cambridge: Cambridge University Press.

Lefebvre, H. (2003) *The Urban Revolution*. Minneapolis, MN: University of Minnesota Press.

Lenz, R. (2010) *Mobilitäten in Europa: Migration und Tourismus auf Kreta und Zypern im Kontext des europäischen Grenzregimes*. Wiesbaden: VS Verlag für Sozialwissenschaften.

Le Page, R.B. (1988) Some premises concerning the standardization of languages, with special reference to Caribbean creole English. *International Journal of the Sociology of Language* 71, 25–36.

Le Page, R.B. and Tabouret-Keller, A. (1985) *Acts of Identity: Creole-Based Approaches to Language and Ethnicity*. Cambridge: Cambridge University Press.

Liddicoat, A.J. (2009) Evolving ideologies of the intercultural in Australian multicultural and language education policy. *Journal of Multilingual and Multicultural Development* 30, 189–203.

Lindsey, T. (2008) Australia 2020 summit. Australia's future in the world. Available at http://www.slidefinder.net/a/australia_history_significant_development_partner/32847405, slide 6 (accessed 21 February 2014)

Lippi-Green, R. (1997) *English with an Accent*. New York: Routledge.

Lipsitz, G. (1994) *Dangerous Crossroads: Popular Music, Postmodernism and the Poetics of Place*. London: Verso.

Lo Bianco, J. (2001) From policy to anti-policy: How fear of language rights took policy-making out of community hands. In J. Lo Bianco and R. Wickert (ed.) *Australian Policy Activism in Language and Literacy* (pp. 13–44). Melbourne: Language Australia.

Lo Bianco, J. (2003) *A Site for Debate, Negotiation and Contest of National Identity: Language Policy in Australia*. Strasbourg: Language Policy Division, Council of Europe.

Lo Bianco, J. (2008) Language policy and education in Australia. In S. May and N. Hornberger (eds) *Encyclopedia of Language and Education* (pp. 343–353). New York: Springer.

Lo Bianco, J. and Australian Department of Education (1987) *National Policy on Languages*. Canberra: Australian Government Publishing Service.

Lopez, M. (2000) *The Origins of Multiculturalism in Australian Politics 1945–1975*. Melbourne: Melbourne University Press.

Makoni, S. and Pennycook, A. (2007) Disinventing and reconstituting languages. In S. Makoni and A. Pennycook (eds) *Disinventing and Reconstituting Languages* (pp. 1–41). Clevedon: Multilingual Matters.

Manuel, P. (1995) *Caribbean Currents: Caribbean Music from Rumba to Reggae*. Philadelphia, PA: Temple University Press.

Marcus, G.E. (1998) Ethnography in/of the world system: The Emergence of multi-sited ethnography. In G.E. Marcus (ed.) *Ethnography Through Thick and Thin* (pp. 79–104). Princeton, NJ: Princeton University Press.

May, S. (2001) *Language and Minority Rights: Ethnicity, Nationalism and the Politics of Language*. London: Longman.

McHoul, A. (2001) Discourse. In R. Meshtrie (ed.) *Concise Encyclopedia of Sociolinguistics* (pp. 133–145). Amsterdam: Elsevier.
McNamara, T. and Shohamy, E. (2008) Language tests and human rights. *International Journal of Applied Linguistics* 18, 89–95.
McPherson, A. (2006) *Anti-Americanism in Latin America and the Caribbean*. New York: Berghahn Books.
Meyerhoff, M. (2003) Communities of practice. In J.K. Chambers, P. Trudgill and N. Schilling-Estes (eds) *The Handbook of Language Variation and Change* (pp. 1–16). Oxford: Blackwell.
Mills, S. (1997) *Discourse*. London: Routledge.
Milroy, L. (1987) *Language and Social Networks*. Oxford: Blackwell.
Möllering, M. (2010) The changing scope of German citizenship: From 'guest-worker' to citizen? In C. Slade and M. Möllering (eds) *From Migrant to Citizen: Testing Language, Testing Culture* (pp. 145–163). Basingstoke: Palgrave Macmillan.
Motschenbacher, H. (2011) Taking queer linguistics further: Sociolinguistics and critical heteronormativity research. *International Journal of the Sociology of Language* 212, 149–179.
Muehlmann, S. and Duchêne, A. (2007) Beyond the nation-state: International agencies as new sites of discourses on bilingualism. In M. Heller (ed.) *Bilingualism: A Social Approach* (pp. 96–110). Basingstoke: Palgrave Macmillan.
New Oxford American Dictionary (2009) Oxford: Oxford University Press.
Ogbar, J.O.G. (2004) *Black Power: Radical Politics and African American Identity*. Baltimore, MD: Johns Hopkins University Press.
Ogbu, J. and Simons, H.D. (1998) Voluntary and involuntary minorities: A cultural–ecological theory of school performance with some implications for education. *Anthropology and Education Quarterly* 2, 155–188.
Ong, A. (1999) *Flexible Citizenship: The Cultural Logics of Transnationality*. Durham, NC: Duke University Press.
Otsuji, E. and Pennycook, A. (2009) Metrolingualism: Fixity, fluidity and language in flux. *International Journal of Multilingualism* 7 (3), 240–254.
Ozolins, U. (1993) *The Politics of Language in Australia*. Cambridge: Cambridge University Press.
Paltridge, B. (2006) *Discourse Analysis*. London: Continuum.
Papadopoulos, M. (2003) Salsa no tiene frontera. Eine Szene ohne Grenzen? In S. Bergmann and R. Römhild (eds) *Global Heimat: Ethnographische Recherchen im transnationalen Frankfurt* (pp. 75–104). Frankfurt am Main: Notizen.
Papastergiadis, N. (2000) *The Turbulence of Migration: Globalization, Deterritorialization, and Hybridity*. Cambridge: Polity Press.
Pavlenko, A. and Piller, I. (2001) New directions in the study of multilingualism, second language learning, and gender. In A. Pavlenko, A. Blackledge, I. Piller and M. Teutsch-Dwyer (eds) *Multilingualism, Second Language Learning, and Gender* (pp. 17–52). Berlin: de Gruyter.
Pennycook, A. (1998) *English and the Discourses of Colonialism*. London: Routledge.
Pennycook, A. (2001) *Critical Applied Linguistics*. Mahwah, NJ: Erlbaum Publishers.
Pennycook, A. (2003) Global Englishes, rip slyme and performativity. *Journal of Sociolinguistics* 7, 513–533.
Pennycook, A. (2004) Performativity and language studies. *Critical Inquiry in Language Studies* 1, 1–19.
Pennycook, A. (2007) *Global Englishes and Transcultural Flows*. London: Routledge.

Pennycook, A. (2010) *Language as a Local Practice*. London: Routledge.

Perez-Stable, M. (1998) *The Cuban Revolution: Origins, Course, and Legacy*. Oxford: Oxford University Press.

Pfadenhauer, M. (2005) Ethnography of scenes: Towards a sociological life-world analysis of (post-traditional) community-building. Paper on Forum Qualitative Sozialforschung/Forum: Qualitative Social Research, at www.qualitative-research.net/index.php/fqs/article/view/23/50 (accessed 20 February 2014).

Phillipson, R. and Skutnabb-Kangas, T. (1997) Lessons for Europe from language policy in Australia. In M. Pütz (ed.) *Language Choices* (pp. 115–158). Amsterdam: John Benjamins.

Phillipson, R. and Skutnabb-Kangas, T. (1999) Minority language rights. In B. Spolsky (eds) *Concise Encyclopaedia of Educational Linguistics* (pp. 51–54). Amsterdam: Elsevier.

Picó, F. (1986) *Historia General De Puerto Rico*. Río Piedras: Ediciones Huracán.

Pietrobruno, S. (2006) *Salsa and Its Transnational Moves*. Lanham, MD: Lexington Books.

Pike, K. (1954) *Language in Relation to a Unified Theory of the Structure of Human Behavior, Part 1*. Glendale, CA: Summer Institute of Linguistics.

Piller, I. (2001a) Identity constructions in multilingual advertising. *Language in Society* 30, 153–186.

Piller, I. (2001b) Naturalization language testing and its basis in ideologies of national identity and citizenship. *International Journal of Bilingualism* 5, 259–277.

Piller, I. (2010a) English – the non-language. Paper on the website Language on the Move, at www.languageonthemove.com/blog/2010/04/29/english-the-non-language (accessed 10 March 2014).

Piller, I. (2010b) Multilingual diversity marketing. Paper on the website Language on the Move, at www.languageonthemove.com/recent-posts/multilingual-diversity-marketing (accessed 10 March 2014).

Piller, I. (2012) Multilingualism and social exclusion. In M. Martin-Jones, A. Blackledge and A. Creese (eds) *Handbook of Multilingualism* (pp. 281–296). London: Routledge.

Piller, I. and Cho, J. (2013) Neoliberalism as language policy. *Language in Society* 42, 23–44.

Pratt, M.L. (1987) Linguistic utopias. In N. Fabb, D. Attridge, A. Durant and C. MacCabe (eds) *The Linguistics of Writing* (pp. 48–66). Manchester: Manchester University Press.

Pries, L. (1997) Neue Migration im transnationalen Raum. In L. Pries (ed.) *Transnationale Migration* (pp. 15–44). Baden Baden: Nomos.

Pries, L. (2001) *Internationale Migration*. Bielefeld: Transcript Verlag.

Pries, L. (2008) *Die Transnationalisierung der sozialen Welt. Sozialräume Jenseits von Nationalgesellschaften*. Frankfurt am Main: Suhrkamp.

Pujolar, J. (2007) Bilingualism and the nation-state in the post-national era. In M. Heller (ed.) *Bilingualism: A Social Approach* (pp. 71–95). Basingstoke: Palgrave Macmillan.

Ramelow, B. (ed.) (2012) *Made in Thüringen¿ Nazi-Terror und Verfassungsschutz-Skandal*. Hamburg: VSA Verlag.

Rampton, B. (1995a) *Crossing: Language and Ethnicity Among Adolescents*. London: Longman.

Rampton, B. (1995b) Language Crossing and the Problematisation of Ethnicity and Socialization. *Pragmatics* 5, 485–513.

Rampton, B. (1997) *Sociolinguistics and Cultural Studies: New Ethnicities, Liminality and Interaction*. Working Papers in Urban Language and Literacies 4, King's College London. Available at www.kcl.ac.uk/sspp/departments/education/research/ldc/publications/workingpapers/download.aspx (accessed 20 February 2014).

Rampton, B. (2000a) Crossing. *Journal of Linguistic Anthropology* 9, 54–56.

Rampton, B. (2000b) *Speech Community*. Working Papers in Urban Language and Literacies 15, King's College London. Available at www.kcl.ac.uk/sspp/departments/education/research/ldc/publications/workingpapers/download.aspx (accessed 10 March 2014).

Rampton, B. (2006) *Language in Late Modernity*. Cambridge: Cambridge University Press.

Rampton, B., Tusting, K., Maybin, J., Barwell, R., Creese, A. and Lytra, V. (2004) *UK Linguistic Ethnography: A Discussion Paper*. Available at www.uklef.net/linguisticethnography.html (accessed 20 February 2014).

Reißlandt, C. (2006) Fit für die Globalisierung? Die Deutsche Migrations- und Integrationspolitik nach den rot-grünen Reformen. In C. Butterwege and G. Hentges (eds) *Zuwanderung im Zeichen der Globalisierung: Migrations-, Integrations- und Minderheitenpolitik* (pp. 135–161). Wiesbaden: VS Verlag für Sozialwissenschaften.

Risager, K. (2006) *Language and Culture: Global Flows and Local Complexities*. Clevedon: Multilingual Matters.

Robertson, R. (1992) *Globalization: Social Theory and Global Culture*. London: Sage.

Rodó, J.E. (1900) Ariel. Available at www.analitica.com/bitblioteca/rodo/ariel.asp (accessed 10 March 2014).

Rodríguez Monegal, E. (1980) La utopía modernista: El mito del nuevo y el viejo mundo en Darío y Rodó. *Revista Iberoamericana* 46, 427–442.

Romaine, S. (2007) Linguistic diversity and language standardization. In M. Hellinger and A. Pauwels (eds) *Handbook of Language and Communication: Diversity and Change* (pp. 685–713). Berlin: de Gruyter.

Román-Velázquez, P. (2002) The making of a salsa music scene in London. In L. Waxer (ed.) *Situating Salsa: Global Markets and Local Meanings in Latin Popular Music* (pp. 259–288). New York: Routledge.

Römhild, R. (2007) Alte Träume, Neue Praktiken: Migration und Kosmopolitismus an den Grenzen Europas. In Transit Migration Forschungsgruppe, *Turbulente Ränder: Neue Perspektiven auf Migration an den Grenzen Europas* (pp. 211–228). Bielefeld: Transcript Verlag.

Rumsey, A. (1990) Word, meaning, and linguistic ideology. *American Anthropologist* 92, 346–361.

Said, E. (1978) *Orientalism*. Harmondsworth: Penguin.

Santos Febres, M. (1997) Salsa as translocation. In C. Fraser Delgado and J. Esteban Muñoz (eds) *Everynight Life: Culture and Dance in Latin/o America* (pp. 175–188). Durham, NC: Duke University Press.

Sarrazin, T. (2010.) *Deutschland schafft sich ab: Wie wir unser Land aufs Spiel setzen*. Munich: Deutsche Verlags-Anstalt.

Saussure, F. de. (1913) [1993]) *Cours de linguistique générale* [*Course in General Linguistics*]. London: Duckworth.

Schiffrin, D., Tannen, D. and Hamilton, H.E. (2001) Introduction. In D. Schiffrin, D. Tannen and H.E. Hamilton (eds) *The Handbook of Discourse Analysis* (pp. 1–10). Oxford: Blackwell.

Schneider, B. (2013a) Heteronormativity and queerness in transnational heterosexual salsa communities. *Discourse and Society* 24, 621–630.

Schneider, B. (2013b) 'In salsa, it's okay to be a woman'. Legitimating heteronormativity in a culturally 'other' environment. *Journal of Language and Sexuality* 2, 262–291.

Schneider, B. (in press) 'Oh boy, ¿hablas español?' – Salsa and the multiple value of authenticity in late capitalism. In T. Breyer, J. Leimgrunber and V. Lacoste (eds) *Indexing Authenticity*. Berlin/New York: de Gruyter.

Silverstein, M. (1979) Language structure and linguistic ideology. In P.R. Clyne, W.F. Hanks and C.L. Hofbauer (eds) *The Elements: A Parasession on Linguistic Units and Levels* (pp. 193–247). Chicago, IL: Chicago Linguistics Society.

Silverstein, M. (2000) Whorfianism and the linguistic imagination of nationality. In P.V. Kroskrity (ed.) *Regimes of Language: Ideologies, Polities and Identities* (pp. 85–138). Santa Fe, NM: School of American Research Press.

Silverstein, M. (2003) Indexical order and the dialectics of sociolinguistic life. *Language and Communication* 23, 193–229.

Skutnabb-Kangas, T. (2000) *Linguistic Genocide in Education – Or Worldwide Diversity and Human Rights?* Mahwah, NJ: Lawrence Erlbaum Associates.

Slade, C. and Möllering, M. (2010) *From Migrant to Citizen: Testing Language, Testing Culture*. Basingstoke: Palgrave Macmillan.

Solimano, A. and Watts, N. (2005) International migration, capital flows and the global economy: A long run view. *Macroeconomía del desarollo* 35, 1–37.

Sonntag, S.K. (2009) Linguistic globalization and the call center industry: Imperialism, hegemony or cosmopolitanism? *Language Policy* 8, 5–25.

Spiegel Online (2006) Schüler begrüßen Deutsch-Pflicht. *Spiegel Online*, 23 January, at www.spiegel.de/schulspiegel/0,1518,396842,00.html (accessed 20 February 2014).

Spivak, G.C. (1996 [1985]) Subaltern studies: Deconstructing historiography. In D. Landry and G. MacLean (eds) *The Spivak Reader* (pp. 203–236). London: Routledge.

Stevenson, P. and Mar-Molinero, C. (eds) (2006a) *Language Ideologies, Policies and Practices: Language and the Future of Europe*. Basingstoke: Palgrave Macmillan.

Stevenson, P. and Mar-Molinero, C. (2006b) Language, the national and the transnational in contemporary Europe. In P. Stevenson and C. Mar-Molinero (eds) *Language Ideologies, Policies and Practices: Language and the Future of Europe* (pp. 1–10). Basingstoke: Palgrave Macmillan.

Stevenson, P. and Schanze, L. (2009) Language, migration and citizenship in Germany: Discourses on integration and belonging. In G. Extra, P. van Avermaet and M. Spotti (eds) *Language Testing, Migration and Citizenship: Cross-National Perspectives on Integration Regimes* (pp. 87–106). London: Continuum.

Stewart, G. (2000) *Rumba on the River: A History of the Popular Music of the Two Congos*. London: Verso.

Takahashi, K. (2013) *Language Learning, Gender and Desire: Japanese Women on the Move*. Bristol: Multilingual Matters.

Turner, V. (1974) Liminal to liminoid in play, flow, and ritual: An essay in comparative symbology. *Rice University Studies* 60, 53–92.

Unesco (1953) *The Use of Vernacular Languages in Education*. Paris: Unesco.

Urry, J. (2007) *Mobilities*. Cambridge: Polity Press.

US Department of Education (2001) No Child Left Behind Act. Available at http://www2.ed.gov/policy/elsec/leg/esea02/107-110.pdf (accessed 20 February 2014).

Vertovec, S. (2007) Super-diversity and its implications. *Ethnic and Racial Studies* 30, 1024–1054.

Vertovec, S. (2010) Towards post-multiculturalism? Changing communities, contexts and conditions of diversity. *International Social Science Journal* 199, 83–95.

Waxer, L. (2002a) Llegó la salsa: The rise of salsa in Venezuela and Colombia. In L. Waxer (ed.) *Situating Salsa: Global Markets and Local Meanings in Latin American Popular Music* (pp. 219–246). New York: Routledge.

Waxer, L. (2002b) Situating salsa: Latin music at the crossroads. In L. Waxer (ed.) *Situating Salsa: Global Markets and Local Meanings in Latin Popular Music* (pp. 3–22). New York: Routledge.

Williams, G. (1999) *French Discourse Analysis: The Method of Post-Structuralism*. London: Routledge.

Williams, G. (2010) *The Knowledge Economy, Language and Culture*. Bristol: Multilingual Matters.

Williams, R. (1966) *Culture and Society, 1780–1950*. New York: Harper & Row.

Williams, R. (1977) *Marxism and Literature*. Oxford: Oxford University Press.

Wimmer, A. and Schiller, N.G. (2002) Methodological nationalism and beyond: Nation-state building, migration and the social sciences. *Global Networks* 2, 301–334.

Wirth, U. (2002) Der Performanzbegriff im Spannungsfeld von Illokution, Iteration und Indexikalität. In U. Wirth (ed.) *Performanz: Zwischen Sprachphilosophie und Kulturwissenschaften* (pp. 9–60). Frankfurt am Main: Suhrkamp.

Wolff, D. (2007) Zur Geschichte und zum gegenwärtigen Stand des bilingualen Sachfachunterrichts in Deutschland. Paper on the website of the Goethe Institute, at www.goethe.de/ges/spa/dos/ifs/cdl/de2747735.htm (accessed 20 February 2014).

Woolard, K.A. (1994) Language ideology. *Annual Review of Anthropology* 23, 55–82.

Woolard, K.A. (1998) Introduction: Language ideology as field of inquiry. In B.B. Schieffelin, K.A. Woolard and P.V. Kroskrity (eds) *Language Ideologies: Practice and Theory* (pp. 3–47). Oxford: Oxford University Press.